W9-CLN-790

THE
COMPLETE
TAO TE CHING
with
THE FOUR CANONS
of the
YELLOW EMPEROR

THE
COMPLETE
TAO TE CHING
with
THE FOUR CANONS
of the
YELLOW EMPEROR

Translation and Commentary by
JEAN LEVI

English Translation by
JODY GLADDING

Inner Traditions
Rochester, Vermont • Toronto, Canada

Inner Traditions
One Park Street
Rochester, Vermont 05767
www.InnerTraditions.com

Library of Congress Cataloging-in-Publication Data

Laozi.
 [Dao de jing. English]
 The complete Tao te ching with the Four canons of the Yellow Emperor / translation and commentary by Jean Levi ; English translation by Jody Gladding. — 1st U.S. ed.
  p. cm.
 Originally published in French under title: Le Lao-tseu suivi des Quatre Canons de l'empereur Jaune. Paris : Éditions Albin Michel, 2009.
 Includes index.
 ISBN 978-1-59477-359-4 (hardcover)
 I. Levi, Jean. II. Gladding, Jody, 1955– III. Huangdi si jing. English. IV. Title.
 BL1900.L26E5 2011
 299.5'1482—dc22

                                                                              2010039540

Printed and bound in the United States by Lake Book Manufacturing

10 9 8 7 6 5 4 3 2 1

Text design and layout by Priscilla Baker
This book was typeset in Garamond Premier Pro with Copperplate used as a display typeface

This work, published as part of a program of aid for publication, received support from CulturesFrance and the French Ministry of Foreign Affairs.

Cet ouvrage a bénéficié du soutien des Programmes d'aide à la publication de CulturesFrance/Ministère français des affaires étrangères et européennes.

CONTENTS

TAO TE CHING:
THE BOOK OF THE WAY
AND OF VIRTUE

THE FOUR CANONS OF THE YELLOW EMPEROR

INTRODUCTION

The textual history of the *Tao Te Ching* is extraordinarily complex and controversial. Even the author's identity is as elusive as the Tao itself, as his name, Lao Tzu, means simply "the old master," an honorific title paying tribute to his old age. Other names attributed to him—the personal name Erh, "ears," and social name Tan, "long ears"—also connote longevity, as old sages were distinguished by the length of their earlobes.

A legend soon grew around this void, beginning largely with the anecdotes in which Lao Tzu appears in the *Chuang Tzu.** A native of Ch'ou, by the name of Li, he was supposed to have been an archivist for the Chou royal court with whom Confucius visited and had a memorable exchange regarding ritual. Then, faced with the display of decadence in the Chou royal house, he supposedly abandoned his post to go west as far as the land of Ch'in. There, at the request of Yin Hsi, who guarded the Han-kou pass, he wrote down the essence of his doctrine in a book with two parts, comprising only five thousand characters, leaving it with him before disappearing without a trace. Following ancient tradition, his name provided the title for the

---

*[The *Chuang Tzu* is a text known by the name of its author, about whom also little is known, beyond the central fact of his being the disciple of Lao Tzu who eloquently developed and expressed the doctrines of Taoism. —*Ed.*]

1

work, the *Lao Tzu,* which later came to be called the *Tao Te Ching* or the *Book of the Way and of Virtue.*

Beginning with these bits of legend and a few clues drawn from scattered historical sources, and looking to recent archaeological discoveries for support, Chinese scholars have tried to reconstruct the genesis of the work. A certain Lao Tan who was an archivist for the Chou court at the end of the Spring and Autumn Period—that is, about the sixth century BCE—could have written a first draft of the *Tao Te Ching.* This ancient account is corroborated by manuscripts on bamboo strips exhumed from a fourth-century BCE tomb in Guodian in 1993 bearing adjacent extracts of some passages from the *Book of the Way and of Virtue.* Then, two centuries later in the Warring States Period, another figure, Tan, the great Chou historian who had an audience with King Hsien of Ch'in (384–361 BCE), may have added passages of his own and revised certain of his precursor's chapters to make them agree with his own views. The Han* version of the *Lao Tzu* may have resulted from these revisions, to which other contributions may have been added and thus, through successive modifications, been transmitted down to us.

Needless to say, ingenious as it is, this scholarly reconstruction, as well as all the concurrent ones that have been proposed, is as fantastic as the hagiographic traditions reported in the first century BCE by the Han historian Szu-ma Ch'ien. It nevertheless has the merit of conforming to the process of division necessarily at work within the universe, since the elusive unity of the figure of Lao Tzu splits into two distinct indi-

---

*[Han refers to the second imperial dynasty of China (206 BCE–220 CE). —*Ed.*]

viduals, who give birth to the *Book,* which will be the source of multiple editions, accompanied by infinite exegeses, in the way that the Two is born of the One to produce the Three, which is nothing other than the engendering power of reality giving rise to the proliferation of the ten thousand beings. In truth, all that can be said of the *Tao Te Ching,* whose author's identity will ever remain unknown to us, is that it is the product of a slow accretion of various materials, combined in a thoughtful, harmonious way, into a sequence of aphorisms that, disparate as they are, nevertheless constitute a coherent whole.

Thus, if the signified idea of the *Book of the Way and of Virtue* is unique, it has gone through quite varied realizations, the *Tao Te Ching* having given rise to different textual traditions—the specialists count five principle ones—to which must be added two earlier versions found more recently: the one discovered in Guodian and another (dating to the early second century BCE) that was discovered in Mawangdui in 1973.

The Way and the Law

In Mawangdui, a town close to Changsha in Hunan, a large number of silk manuscripts on many diverse subjects were exhumed from an early Han burial place. Among those documents were two versions of the *Tao Te Ching.* The oldest version, called "version A," a very corrupt one, was written before the appearance of the first Han emperor, Liu Pang, in 206 BCE; the second, called "version B," a bit more recent and better preserved, must have been calligraphed between 194 and 187 BCE. Much older than all existing versions (until the 1993 Guodian find again changed the scenario), these two manuscripts shared the remarkable peculiarity of reversing the order of the parts—in them, the "Book of Virtue" precedes the "Book of the Way"—and of not being divided into chapters as standard editions are, the process of fragmentation inherent in the Way having only begun. While the sentence order in each part generally follows the versions that have come down to us, it does diverge in some places, thus sometimes offering lessons quite far removed from the received texts. For many scholars, it was a matter of an older—and more authentic—*Lao Tzu*.

Most importantly, each of the two versions was accompanied by four previously unknown texts. Version A of the Taoist classic was followed by an appendix of four distinct fragments unrelated to one another. In manuscript B, on the other hand, the *Book of the Way and of Virtue* was preceded by four chapters, which some Chinese scholars believed they were able to identify as *The Four Canons of the Yellow Emperor,* a treatise lost until then, but whose title had been recorded in the bibliographical section of the *Official Annals of the Han Dynasty* under the rubric of Taoist works.

Identifying the four texts that open version B of the Mawangdui *Tao Te Ching* as *The Four Canons of the Yellow Emperor* has the dual advantage of giving them an evocative title and, in labeling them as all one work, emphasizing their thematic and ideological kinship. Yet this all remains purely conjectural. Most importantly it presents the serious inconvenience of explaining the contents of a book by assigning it to a political trend that remains ever vague, because it has nothing to do with a doctrine or a school. Instead, it crystallizes, in the emblematic figure of the Yellow Emperor, the absolutist exercise of power reconsidered within the framework of Taoist presuppositions. Still, it does provide a possible explanation and clarification of an expression that appears frequently in the writings of Han historians: "Ho-kang-Lao school." This expression designates a political doctrine much in vogue at the beginning of the dynasty, inspired by the philosophy known as Legalism* crossed with Taoism. In the term *Ho-kang-Lao, Ho-kang* refers to writings under the patronage of the Yellow Emperor (Huang Ti)—for which the newly discovered texts provided a prototype—and *Lao* refers to the doctrine laid out in the *Book of the Way and of Virtue,* attributed to Lao Tzu. The politics inspired by this trend, fruit of an improbable but successful marriage between legalist authoritarianism and Taoist spontaneity, may have ensured peace and prosperity for the early Han empire and established the foundations of its power.

Even though, given the current state of documentation, it is impossible to offer definitive proof that the four texts form a whole, thematic ties and ideological unity exist nevertheless, leading us to consider them as constituting a single homogenous entity. Moreover, it seems that the arrangement of the sections reveals a conscious attempt at organization. The last text, "The Original Way" (designated as canon IV), is a cosmogonic amplification of the first section of canon I, entitled "The Law Way." At the same time it provides a condensed version of the substance of the three preceding sections. The two

---

*[The legalist philosophy promoted the absolutist power of the ruler, supported by laws, as a counter to the evil considered to be inherent in human nature. —*Ed.*]

titles (of the first section of canon I and of canon IV) correspond to each other word for word: *Tao Fa* is both "The Law
of the Tao" (or "The Law Way") and "The Tao as the Law"
(or "The Way as Law"), and the chapter attempts to depict
the Way when it is manifested in an effective form in human
institutions and in the prince's art of governing; similarly, the
title of canon IV, *Tao Yuan*, means both "The Origin of the
Tao" and "The Tao as Origin," or alternatively, the Way taken
in its cosmogonic dimension of primordial entity, born before
Heaven and Earth, anterior to Creation, and considered in its
activity of engendering all beings. The book thus opens and
closes with two symmetrical geneses. Even though the genesis
of social law by the Tao seems limited to the earthly sphere,
it actually harbors a cosmic dimension, because social law is
never more than the diffraction of the ontological dynamism
into human affairs, and as such, it engenders order.

The Tao is both the source of Law and the origin of Being.
If the Law has a transcendent quality as an expression of the
final Principle, the final Principle is ultimately absorbed into
the action of the sage who brings order to the empire. After
lyrically evoking Non-Being giving birth to Being, the last of
the four canons, "The Original Way," closes with a description of the sovereign's regulating function, so that through
this alternating movement, the Principle is embodied in the
prince and the prince merges into the Tao.

The law enforced by the sovereign is not at all an arbitrary,
human construction, issuing from a contract between free and
equal subjects, but the realization in society of the Principle
itself, which, in contact with humans, from Way becomes Law.
The Law still draws its validity from seasonal cycles and the

regular trajectory of the stars. Punishment and reward compare respectively to autumn when things perish and to spring when things prosper. The metaphor is woven into a whole system of correspondences in another section of the first canon, titled "Summary of the Great Principles." To have the force of Law, social and historical laws must possess the same properties as the cosmological Heaven: exactitude, regularity, clarity, conformity, unicity.

If nature obeys unvarying laws, they will be at work in humans even as they are in the turning of the seasons. Thus they are manifested in what is called "human nature," which amounts to instincts and passions. Government is a kind of training. It imprints unconscious behaviors on humans in place of, or rather as extensions of, instincts. Permeating the social body and in some way inherent in the territorial organization that allows its enforcement, this law finds its source in the transcendence of the prince. This transcendence is affirmed by the operation consisting of giving "names" to "forms," that is, appointing positions as a function of tasks and achievements. The sovereign worthy of this name invests no individual will. He is content to establish within human society an ineluctable necessity obtained through absolute, unobstructed application of the Law that is clearly nothing but the socialized form of the Way.

This dual aspect of the Law, conforming both to the instincts immanent in the species and to the standards of transcendent astronomy that rule the planets, also appears in the pair of antithetical ideas of *ni,* "contrary to the order," and *shuan,* "in accordance with the order," which are very difficult to translate because of the many levels on which they operate.

Equally within the frameworks of individual behavior, state policy, and astronomical phenomena, they sanction conformity or nonconformity to good rule or reason. They could almost be translated as "good" and "bad," when they describe behavior, but behavior tending downward toward the instincts and upward toward the natural course of things, so that they have the quasi-physiological connotations of the normal and the pathological on the one hand, and the quasi-cosmological connotations of the regular and the aberrant on the other; furthermore, applied to the activities of conscious thought, they sanction the rationality or irrationality of decisions and attitudes. Moreover, they have an ethical dimension to the extent that they name a transcendent retribution. Through this pair of opposites the close solidarity of the two orders, human and heavenly, is manifested, because corresponding to any social deviance there is necessarily a natural deviance, insofar as the art of governing becomes an art of conforming to the course of things and the art of being a subject to a spontaneous reflex of obedience to the edicts of the monarch.

Taoist Philosophy and the *Tao Te Ching*

When presenting readers with philosophical concepts belonging to another civilization unfamiliar to them, it is customary to begin with a general account of the main ideas, even if it means filling in the details afterward. That is more or less the way all specialists have proceeded until now when explaining to novices some aspect or line of Chinese thought: Confucianism, Legalism, Moism, or Taoism. But we may wonder if such a procedure is appropriate for the last of these. I am very much afraid that by adopting this expository mode, we risk letting what constitutes the essence of Taoism escape, judging at least by the frustration that all the general studies on Taoism I have read have prompted in me, however remarkable their authors may be otherwise. Undoubtedly this stems from the very particular nature of the Tao and from the line of thought that is its object for reflection.

We could say about the Tao what Dante said of the Italian language: like the odiferous panther, its scent is everywhere and its home nowhere. We find Taoism in a more or less concentrated form in all of the ancient Chinese philosophies, but none can properly be called "Taoist" insofar as there exists no school or Taoist doctrine compiled before the late second century CE, the period in which the sect of the Celestial Masters appeared. Moreover, we can trace improbable lineages and discover vague affinities between certain thinkers and certain writings, often anonymous or apocryphal. But the Tao, to which all the ancient philosophies look for authority to a greater or lesser extent, is a notion so contradictory and evanescent that it thwarts any attempt at definition. Or more, in the works that retroactively constitute the Taoist canon, it is presented as eluding all characterization by its very nature. Through the words of one of his allegorical figures, "Without Beginning," Chuang Tzu pronounces this irrevocable judgment: "The Tao cannot be understood: what is understood is not the Tao; the Tao cannot be perceived: what is perceived is not the Tao; the Tao cannot be expressed: what is expressed is not the Tao." And the reason for this: "What gives form to the forms is without form. The Tao answers to no name."

Which way to go, then, to get back to it? Perhaps by taking

the opposite approach, by beginning with the exegesis of a model passage—from a dialogue or a fable, for example, since those are two forms of expression favored by the thinkers categorized as "Taoists"—like a thread to follow through the maze of contradictory meanings, uncertain categories, and cryptic expressions. Among all the parables and anecdotes that comprise the writings of the "Taoist Fathers," is there any more appropriate for approaching the Tao than that fable from the *Lieh Tzu** that tries to put its reader on the right path through the story of getting lost? I mean the famous parable of the philosopher and the stray sheep. Here is a very free translation of it.

The One and the Many
The Allegory of the Stray Sheep

A neighbor of the philosopher Yang Chu had lost a ewe. He had gathered together all the members of his clan to find it and had even enlisted the master's disciples. Yang Chu was surprised:

"What, so many people for one sheep?"

"That's because there are so many side paths," the farmer explained.

Yang Chu saw them coming back a short time later.

"And so, you've found the animal?" he asked.

"No," said the sheep's owner. "Each fork leads to another fork, and so on, so that very soon, we no longer knew which way to turn, so we gave up."

At these words, Yang Chu grew pale and hurried home.

---

*[The *Lieh Tzu* is, along with the *Lao Tzu* and the *Chuang Tzu,* considered to be one of the three foundational texts of Taoism. —*Ed.*]

He stayed inside, scowling and somber, for many weeks, and his students could not get a word of explanation out of him.

Finally, accompanied by a fellow student, the student most advanced in the Way sought him out and asked him the following question:

"A father had three sons. He sent them to study Confucian virtues with a scholar in Lu. When they returned, he asked them what constituted Goodness and Justice. The eldest son said, 'Goodness and Justice require that one take care of oneself without regard for one's reputation.' The second son said, 'Goodness and Justice require that one be ready to sacrifice oneself in order to gain a reputation.' The youngest son answered, 'Goodness and Justice consist of caring for both oneself and one's reputation.' From the same teaching, the three brothers had drawn different lessons. Which of the three was right?"

Yang Chu answered, "There was a man who lived beside a river and had grown used to water when he was very small. He had become an excellent swimmer and rowed with great skill. He had even made it his trade, since he carried travelers in his boat from one shore to the other in return for payment. That was how he could provide for the needs of his large family and bring in a modest living. He soon attracted a throng of students. Nearly half of them drowned. Nevertheless, all of them had come to him to learn to swim, not to learn to drown. Considering the results, who was right and who was wrong?"

The disciple remained silent and left. The other student who had accompanied him exploded in anger:

"What's the point of these tortuous questions and evasive answers? Now I'm further behind than I was before!"

"Nevertheless, it's clear," the first student said, "that the sheep was lost because of the many forks in the road. Likewise scholars waste their lives in the proliferation of doctrines. Although they have one common origin, through transmission they diverge completely. Only one who finds his identity in returning to unity will avoid getting lost. You've been the master's student and practiced his doctrine for a long time, and you still can't understand his great lines. What a shame!"

Such is the depth of Chinese fables: they always speak to us through enigmas, and what elucidation they claim to provide turns out to be a new enigma, even more impenetrable, so that we would be tempted to applaud this fable's bad disciple and exclaim, "Here we are even further behind than before!" as if our uncomprehending reaction were itself included in the equation and constituted a key element of it. Obscurity is precisely what allows revelation, in the very degree to which it manifests what cannot be revealed, because truth—insofar as we can speak of truth—derives from what is revealed not through discourse but in the everyday appearance of things that allows us to see, humbly—we might be tempted to say bucolically—a stray sheep that is never found again, for example.

Thus the anecdote is presented in the form of a series of interrogations whereby each subsequent one, while claiming to explain the preceding one, gives rise to a new question, in such a way that, far from offering illumination, it only deepens the mystery and increases our perplexity. In fact, the solution is given not by the final word—the disciple, as we will see, explains nothing—but by the deployment of these questions into narrative space, which somehow mirrors the process recounted by the fable, thus signifying that this is the only legitimate way to speak of the Way. In this sense, it is a magnificent example of what the ancients called "subtle words," illustrated by the following anecdote from a third-century BCE philosophical encyclopedia:

> *Prince P'ei, who wanted to incite a rebellion, sought Confucius to get his advice and asked, "Can disguised words be understood?"*
>
> *Confucius did not answer. The prince insisted, "If someone throws a stone into the water, what then?"*
>
> *"Diving in after it is enough," answered Confucius.*
>
> *"And if one throws water into the water?"*
>
> *"I Ya the cook could distinguish by taste the waters of the Ch'u and the waters of the Sheng where they flow together."*
>
> *"Then it is no use resorting to allusive words?"*
>
> *"Who said so? But first you must know the true meaning of the words."*

From this the author draws the following lesson: "The one who knows the meaning of the word does not need to resort to the word that is never more than its appendix. If one gets soaked catching fish and chases after game, it is not for pleasure but from necessity. That is why the supreme word abolishes the word, the supreme action is non-action. Alas, a superficial intelligence only becomes attached to the inessential. That is the reason why Prince P'ei perished under the law."

Oral expression will never be more than a last resort, a place to turn only when there is no better alternative; it is a kind of admission of powerlessness. Words are not the only means for making oneself understood: there can be silences that hide words; also and above all, there can be a silence that is equivalent to a word. Confucius's silence in the face of his interlocutor is eloquent, and it takes all the denseness of a Prince P'ei not to be able to interpret it.

Better than any discourse, the silence adopted by master Yang Chu following the failed search for the sheep sparks that curiosity prerequisite to all authentic knowledge. Thus, true eloquence would lie in speech that does away with speech, that is, with voice bearing meaning. In some way, the fable of the sheep provides the allegorical transcription of the Taoist maxim: "The one who knows does not talk, the one who talks does not know, that is why the sage practices teaching without words." It might also explain, imagistically, the enigmatic opening phrase of the first section in standard editions of the *Tao Te Ching*, interpreted various ways, but, many and diverse as they are, all coming back to questioning the efficacy of discourse: "The way given voice is not the true Way."

It goes without saying that the loss of the sheep does not prompt the philosopher's torment, but rather the allegorical interpretation that he cannot fail to draw from it. However, the legend seems to be flawed in that once Yang Chu sinks into silence, no one in his entourage truly understands what is going on, although they all remain convinced that it is a matter of the greatest importance. Is that because they are deprived of the master's speech, which constitutes, if not their reason to be, at least their reason to be in his presence? Which also means that the loss of the sheep has an allegorical dimension only to the extent that it is accompanied by the master's silence. Since the value of an allegory inheres only in the lesson to be drawn from it, the fable of the ewe thus appears a kind of anti-fable.

The parable of the three brothers offered by the disciple to his master aims at remedying that explanatory vacuum. Instead of asking directly about his strange reaction, as any philistine would, the disciple displays his mastery over allusive speech and tries to worm the information out of his master obliquely through means of an allegory that already proposes an answer even though it is presented in the form of a question; in effect, he suggests that his master's despondency over the lost sheep has allowed him to realize the vanity of any transmission of knowledge through language. If the lesson is singular, its reception is plural: the truth is diffracted into a multitude of partial opinions—a function of individual subjectivity—so that, just as paths branch infinitely, doctrines multiply until it proves impossible to know where the truth lies. Note that even if the disciple exposes the contradictions, he can imagine nothing other than Confucian teaching: he chooses the conventional example of the literati of Lu (Confucius's ancient homeland), in which two pillars of Confucian doctrine, Goodness and Justice, serve as his subject for divergent interpretations. Even while pointing out the limits of the literati tradition, the disciple makes it the ultimate framework for all teaching and all transmission of knowledge, just as he poses its moral categories as the only ones containing knowledge.

Thus the master must provide a clarification. The disciple's fable, skillfully—and perhaps impertinently—presented in the form of a question, insidiously questions Yang Chu's teaching by taking a parodic stance toward it (because Yang

Chu's doctrine famously opposes the altruistic virtues of goodness and justice to the individualist cultivation of the self, focused on self-preservation). The master's retort is another fable, presented in the form of a riddle, thanks to which he eludes the trap set by the disciple and, demonstrating that he is still the master, silences his student and gets the last word. But above all, he manages a subtle shift in the equation that completely alters the perspective and finally undermines his disciple's ideological presuppositions, without the disciple realizing it, presuppositions that led precisely to his role as disciple to a master who dispenses a constituted body of knowledge.

Yang Chu founded a countermovement to Mo Tzu's altruism,* even while opposing Confucian "humanism"; thus he was involved in the ideological debates of his age and contributed to the cacophony of the schools. Nevertheless, with his lesson, he offers a radical change of scenery: the context for teaching is no longer terrestrial but aquatic; the place of transmission shifts from the classroom or, more accurately, the pathway—most schools being itinerant at that time—to the waterway. In carrying out this substitution, the philosopher (whom the author makes his spokesperson) skillfully employs the system of representations, earth the counterpart of water, the paradigmatic element of Taoism, just as the Confucian cart is opposed to the old fisherman's boat, the embodiment of some Taoist sage in some fable or dialogue from the *Chuang*

---

*[Mo Tzu, a fifth-century BCE philosopher, opposed both Confucianism (by emphasizing self-reflection and authenticity rather than obedience to ritual) and Taoism (by seeing, for example, Heaven as a benevolent, moral force that rewarded good and punished evil rather than as amoral mystical nature). —*Ed.*]

Tzu. But if the river environment provides the primordial scene where true learning and genuine knowledge are manifested, because beyond all language they are in harmony with that environment and with acquisition through permeation, it is also fundamental because of the special status water enjoys in Taoist texts: in the universe of constituted forms, it is the element closest to the Tao; many chapters in the *Lao Tzu* are nothing other than hymns to its glory.

Next, the master replaces the teaching of moral doctrine through speech with learning how to row through practice. Thus, he becomes part of the *Chuang Tzu* tradition that exalts the artisan's expertise, by which the skillful act harbors something as miraculous as the course of nature, or rather by which dexterity proceeds from an intimate understanding of how things function, a knowledge so profoundly integrated into the individual that it is more on the order of instinct than of intellectual activity. Which is also to say that there is no other touchstone for truth than practical efficiency. If true knowledge really consists of notions as vague as goodness and justice, giving rise to perplexity and conjecture, that is not the case for swimming. There, error is immediately sanctioned by experience: you go from life to death.

By replacing both the framework and substance of transmission, the master means to correct what is both too radical and too restrictive about his student's interpretation of his silence. Yes, exactly, the Way is lost in the proliferation of doctrines, but first and foremost, it nonetheless exists, as all empirical experience shows—thus it is enough to trace all the theories back to their shared root through reducing the oppositions—and second, transmission cannot be ensured through speech but only through action. On the strength of this clarification, which he only half understands, the disciple believes he is authorized to pronounce the final word.

In short, the moral of the lost sheep as explained by the disciple would concur with the passage about the malignant proliferation of the hundred schools in the final chapter of the *Chuang Tzu:*

> With the fragmentation of knowledge into many distinct branches, the unity of the Tao was lost from view. The doctrines proliferated and each, delighting in its own truncated apprehension of reality, took a fragmented vision for the whole of knowledge. It is as if each of the senses, hearing, seeing, touch, taste, smell, claimed to encompass all aspects of the perceptible universe, without consulting one another. In the same way, each school, interested only in a thin branch of the tree of knowledge, takes its small specialty for universal knowledge on the pretext that it is useful in given circumstances and offers advantages in some particular area. But these are only fragmentary conceptions of the experiential whole, barely worthy of village literati. The beauty of the world was destroyed in wanting to understand it, the reason for things was dissected, the universal, intuitive knowledge of the Ancients was parceled out. Is it any surprise that under these conditions, the marvels of the universe achieve so little, the Mind in its true splendor encompasses so little?

Nevertheless, nothing obliges us to accept the interpretation of a disciple who will never have more than partial vision of the master's teaching. We could draw an entirely different lesson from the fable of the lost sheep and from the master's enigmatic response to the disciple's question, also presented in the form of a riddle. Interestingly, by refusing to take the disciple's words at face value, we are only conforming to the allegory's moral. The disciple is the first to denounce the reductive nature of any transmission, is he not? The fable contains its own antidote by directing us not to be taken in by proposed explanations, even if it offers them itself. The true meaning of the story exceeds the restrictive interpretation given by the student, even as amended by the master, who broadens its field of application while taking care not to provide any universal overview nor to draw from it any generalizations. Thus if we want to return to the very source of Yang Chu's teaching, we can reject the scholarly, prosaic explanation of the disciple, who as a good disciple thinks only in terms of knowledge and transmission, and apply the master's words to domains far more vast and essential, to how things function in that privileged terrain: life itself.

Moreover, Yang Chu's fable suggests just this, in finding no better discipline to illustrate a model of transmission than an activity as trivial, mundane, and physical as swimming or rowing. Moreover, if it were only a matter of a teaching or doctrine corrupted over centuries, his bout of sadness would be incomprehensible. The ewe's fate has plunged him into true existential crisis, such a crisis that it makes him utter incoherent words and confuse a sage with a boatman and teaching the Way with drowning! If the master is sad, it is because he is afraid of being lost himself and of having wasted his life. Or rather, he understands that one's life, as satisfying as it can seem—Yang Chu is famous, surrounded by a crowd of disciples—is the product of an irremediable loss, as soon as its direction results from a choice. Every choice, insofar as it excludes other choices, narrows the possibilities. Even though the branches apparently multiply, that multiplication of options proportionally diminishes our free will, and our alternatives never cease to dwindle.

The parable must thus be read as the illustrational and, if you will, *topological* transcription of the *Tao Te Ching*'s section 38, which contains the following sequence: "After the loss of the Tao comes Virtue, after the loss of Virtue comes Goodness, after the loss of Goodness comes Justice, after the loss of Justice comes Ritual." This chain reaction, itself a projection, into the ethical human sphere, of that process by which the fragmentation of the unconditioned whole gives rise to the multiplicity of reality, ends in the creative Principle's efficacy dwindling into ever narrower virtues. When the process is over, what remains are the stereotyped behaviors demanded by ceremonial protocol, subsumed into the universal norm of social relationships.

Charity and justice—cleverly appearing under cover of the disciple's allegory—are only simple by-products of the Tao's efficiency, destined to be ossified into ritual. As pure transcendence of form without content, ritual is useless; worse, it is at the source of all conflicts. Reified residue of the ontological dynamism, stripped of all creative power, it can barely exert influence over, much less unite, anyone; to the contrary, its hierarchizing and disruptive effects can only provoke rivalries and conflicts. Ritual is thus condemned because, as the final link in the chain of differentiation, it has lost all transformative power. That is why the author of the *Tao Te Ching* can conclude his sequences on the degradation of the Way with phrases as violent and apparently paradoxical as "Ritual is the husk of faith and the source of disorder," or the even more brutal "supreme Ritual acts and, lacking response, rolls up its sleeves and pummels." In a word, being overly determined renders ritual perfectly ineffective.

Only the void or the unconditioned can create Being; it is the true engine of action and the principle of all existence. Annotating that same section 38, the philosopher Wang Pi explains that only Non-Being, as absolute negativity, can be fertile. As he formulates it: "We must watch over the Mother rather than the Son. Hold to the root rather than the branches." This rhetorical balance, incidentally, simply paraphrases the lines of section 52: "The world has an origin: I call it the Mother of the Tao. Whoever grasps the mother knows the son, whoever knows the son will know how to guard the mother." In less imagistic terms, we must concern ourselves with this first and only origin that makes things *things,* because as pure dynamism and absolute virtuality it is the source of creation, just as the walk matters more than the footprints left by it. Thus goodness and justice produced by the Mother of all things—the "Dark Female Principle of the universe," to use the accepted phrase—can never take the place of the Mother, as they are far too subject to determinations. They are powerless to engender either goodness or equity, and barely able to offer a diminished version in the pitiful form of ritual, in the same way as tools and objects are made by artisans—potters or smiths—but they themselves cannot make things or make artisans.

In short, "that which gives being to beings does not belong to Being." As soon as we abandon the Principle for the product or the effect, we find ourselves cast into the universe of things and names, a sterile world comprised of "made forms" that, having lost all virtuality for the sake of their actuality, are incapable of creating anything whatsoever. All being partakes of the Tao, depending upon it for existence. The Way is the raison d'être for all beings in existence; they are dependent on it and receive from it attributions or virtues that condition them and provide standards for them. The natural state of things, the principle making each thing thus and not otherwise, is that universal presence of the "this by which" things exist, manifested, ensuring that realities remain faithful to their specifications, and spontaneously so, without outside intervention. Reciprocally, the absence of determination gives the Principle its creative power and establishes it as source and support for all that is conditioned. To be One—because at its origin, the Way is One, before branching and being lost in the multiplicity of determined individualities—and to control that burgeoning multiplicity, the Tao must simply appear as the opposite or reverse of all manifested realities, in the face of the multiple. That is, it must figure forth as absolute absence of being and total, ultimate non-realization; it must be Nothing, in short.

To use the words of Chuang Tzu himself, "The Tao is Chao Wen before he plays the zither, Being is Chao Wen as soon as he strikes the zither's strings." As soon as there is a departure from the root or the source from which all realities—which are only realizations or diffractions of the Principle in the divided universe—arise, some measure of effectiveness is lost;

thus each thing, even while it obeys a vital necessity, is the sign of irremediable loss, each option sanctioning a virtuality abandoned. Any first choice leads to a second alternative, which conditions the sequence of other things that follow, and so on until life is over, with no possibility of reversing direction, so that this apparent freedom obeys an absolute necessity.

Therein lies the deep, hidden meaning of the passage, similar to the phrase in the *Lao Tzu*'s section 42, where we find summarized the secret arithmetic of the universe: "The Tao gives birth to the One, the One to the Two, the Two to the Three; from the Three are born the ten thousand beings."

The One and the Many
Content and Form of the Tao Te Ching

From this brief study of an apparently insignificant anecdote consigned to the most minor of the three founding works of early Taoism we have been able to extract three essential themes highlighted by this short passage and informing all Taoist thought: criticism of language as a means for knowing and transmitting how things work, privileging the physical act as an authentic means for such knowledge and transmission, and finally, affirming the oneness of such knowledge reflecting the oneness of its subject, the Tao. It goes without saying that these three themes are closely related. They are nothing more than corollaries for the postulate of the Way's emptiness. Offered in various forms throughout the *Tao Te Ching,* as apparently unrelated cryptic aphorisms, they are actually organized into a system interweaving all the elements.

For the author of the *Book of the Way and of Virtue,* the world in which we live is a world of constructed objects or implements, *ch'i* (or, as the *Chuang Tzu* would say, "made forms," *ch'eng-hsing*), which determine the contents of prefabricated consciousness. This idea is expressed in sections 32 and 28 of the *Tao Te Ching* through the image of wood carved into objects: "The Way has no name because it is rough wood." "Rough wood, carved, provides tools. The sage, put to use, is head of the officials. The supreme Maker never carves anything." The dissipation of phenomena into the fragmented world sanctions the loss of all subjective freedom and ruins the undifferentiated, empty depths of psychic activity. Thus a causal relationship is posited between the opening of the perceptible world and the loss of energies that leads to decay and death.

Thus it makes sense to renounce individual consciousness, to return to a chaotic, precognitive stage, the natural state in which early humanity lived and which still remains that of the newborn: "I am the newborn who has not yet laughed. . . . They know how to do everything, only I am impervious. Why so solitary? Because I still nurse from my mother," it says in the ironic lines of section 20. Present spontaneously in the primitive and the newborn, this state of indistinction must be recovered by civilized humanity. The experience of indistinction assumes first that we detach ourselves from the perceptible world; we create a void by cutting ties with the external environment. Closing the gates of understanding and concentrating our vital spirits makes it possible to keep the channels of perception undifferentiated and our potentialities intact, by leaving them unrealized. In this chaotic state, we possess the embryo's wealth of virtualities, pregnant with all possibilities, since no determination has been chosen: a self-enclosed self-sufficient entity, harboring the chaos and nourishing itself under the warm protective cover of the amniotic sac, totally ignorant of everything, beginning with itself. "Whoever possesses the vital force is like the newborn. . . . His bones are supple, his tendons flexible, and his grip powerful. He knows nothing of sex, but his penis is erect because his vitality is at its height," asserts the *Tao Te Ching* in section 55. Section 49 offers these fine phrases: "The sage is on his guard in society, because he knows how to keep from the outer world the divine confusion he harbors in his heart. Most of us are enslaved by our eyes and ears, while he laughs at them, blissful as a babe."

Thus modes of consciousness exist that lead to modes of unconsciousness. Far from producing lapses in our faculties, they result in a radiant deployment of our vital force, because they make us one with the organic energies and breaths partaking of the universal impulses. It is the transition to such a state of consciousness that section 15 describes: ". . . hesitant as though they were crossing a frozen river, circumspect as though they feared their neighbors, solemn as though paying a visit, they melted like snow in the sun, and then seemed dazed as stumps, troubled as muddy water, gaping as valleys, troubled water that, resting, gradually clears, resting body that, slowly, movement brings back to life. Whoever devotes himself to that art is not seeking fulfillment, not seeking fulfillment, he is endlessly renewed."

Language, with its fixed categories, its hierarchy of values, in short, its logic of classification that establishes arbitrary divisions in what is by nature undivided, cannot encompass the passionate, seething, radiant creation from which the elemental world springs, especially because the Principle is, essentially, mystery, without determinations and thus impossible to qualify and to name. The irreducible nature of the Principle to any form of verbal expression is the *Lao Tzu*'s fundamental postulate: "The way given voice is not the true Way," the first line of the *Book of the Way* affirms. In the true knowledge of the Tao there is a depth of obscurity that both grounds it as authentic knowledge and limits it to approximation of the unknowable and unconditioned.

These "properties" of the Tao call for a particular approach so as not to make it vanish. We can only name it by default, because it is in default of being. Thus it can be suggested only through an alternative language practice and a new mode of writing. The *Tao Te Ching* uses cryptic, incantatory language to describe the ultimate Principle, a language in which ambiguous words unleash a multiplicity of meanings on the multiple levels that constitute the whole field of reality. Even someone like Kafka finds himself helpless before such use of language: "Lao Tzu's aphorisms are impossible nuts to crack," he confided to his young friend Gustav Janouch. "They enchant me but their kernels remain impenetrable to me. I have read them many times, but I find that, like a little boy playing with marbles, I just let them glide from one corner of my thoughts to another without getting anywhere."

Thus, recurring motifs appear throughout the text, in a variety of guises, most often poetic, incantatory, and imagistic embellishments on the dialectic of the One and the many. But if the work's content is entirely animated by this opposition, it escapes its container to command its textual history. Because even if there is a single central idea, the forms in which it has been recorded have varied considerably over time, as have the interpretations given to it. So that, to paraphrase Chuang Tzu, not only has the Way been divided into the various currents that share the empire, but even in the main current bearing the greatest share of the Tao's true heritage, the *Tao Te Ching*, it appears in various guises and gives rise to divergent, even opposing interpretations. The several different textual traditions have in turn divided into multiple sub-variants accompanied by commentaries and sub-commentaries, branching to infinity, like that branching path where the sheep in the *Lieh Tzu* fable was lost. To return to our own sheep, the disciple must certainly see that the Way is lost in the burgeoning of doctrines, but, good emulator of the old master that he is, he observes that "the movement of the Tao is return," given that "creation, an endless carousel, always returns to its root," and thus concludes that it is possible to find the truth again by tracing back to the origin. And since we too think that the lessons of old masters are never to be ignored, why not adopt this precept and trace back through the past to find the doctrine again in its original purity?

In fact, the Han version unearthed in Mawangdui is one step closer to the source, and so in some way more "authentic," even if, insofar as it is only a manifestation of the truth of the text, and not the truth itself, it cannot supply the definitive key to understanding the *Tao Te Ching*. Similarly, *The Four Canons of the Yellow Emperor,* the mystical-political text on the art of absolute government that accompanies it, testifies eloquently to the practical dimension latent in any doctrine, even the most abstract one, in the Warring States Period when all philosophical systems tended toward efficiency. In a certain way, it fits the *Lieh Tzu* allegory's moral perfectly and conforms to Yang Chu's lesson of the boatman and his disciples. Indeed, thanks to the secrets to governing contained there, a prince may navigate the stormy seas of history, steering his craft serenely without sinking body or goods.

The Emptiness of the Sovereign and the Asceticism of the Yellow Emperor

Insofar as he is the source and the guarantor for the Law, the sovereign is identified with the Way. Thus he must devote himself to being empty: he is empty of all desire, empty of all thought, and empty of all intentionality. The sovereign rules his subjects thanks to the law, radiant as yang, and thanks to manipulation techniques, hidden as yin, that free him from dependence on his own talents. This control over others comes through his clear-sightedness. Even though all eyes are turned to him, the sovereign can manipulate others because the proper techniques allow him to see through them. His subjects are transparent to him provided that he is impenetrable to them. It is enough that he appears indifferent, while others are inflated with appetites and possessed by passions. A man without qualities, he offers nothing to others because he is nothing other than the mirror reflecting nothing.

Still, he must possess the secrets for attaining this state. To the outward art of dominating others through their passions is opposed the esoteric art of self-control, consisting of ruling one's appetites, or rather ridding oneself of them. The elimination of desires can only be obtained through practices

inspired by Taoist asceticism, stressed in the second canon of
The Four Canons, "The Great Canonical Rules," devoted to
the Yellow Emperor's mystical act that leads the rebel Ch'e-yu
to repent.

In the myth, the Yellow Emperor acquires preeminence
and can thus serve as a unifying symbol of the many themes of
sovereignty, because as rector of Earth, he reigns over the middle, and that position removes him from the yearly cycle. In
China there are five directions, including the central square,
but there are never more than four seasons, the fifth being
pure dream, the empty point in the circle of time. The Yellow
Emperor occupies the center, but it is an empty center, which
is to say that he plays the role of pivot. And like any pivot,
he fulfills the function of regulation and control. Beginning
from the middle, he establishes the order and harmony that he
dispenses over space to the ends of the world. Removed from
the cycle of changes and principle of their movement for this
very reason, he devotes himself to being the terrestrial, anthro-
pomorphized replica of the Tao—when the Tao embodies the
cosmic regulator in the form of T'ai-yi, the supreme One,
highest divinity in the pantheon, residing in the North Star,
the axis around which the celestial dome moves. This middle
is located on two levels, macrocosmic and microcosmic. First,
on the macrocosmic level, it is identified with the royal palace toward which all information is directed and from which
all civilizing influence emanates in return; second, on the
microcosmic level, it is the heart that maintains equilibrium
among the organs, an equilibrium that reflects in the harmony between the individual and the external environment
and radiates virtue. The final couplet of section 5 of the *Lao*

Tzu expresses this in its abstract, enigmatic way: "Wanting to know everything quickly exhausts you: it is best to occupy the center."

To defeat his rival Ch'e-yu, symbol of wanton violence and disorder, the Yellow Emperor must retreat to the symbolically named "Distant View Mountain" and, by overturning the self through mystical asceticism, become a "pile of dry bones," no longer possessing desire or will, empty of all passion. Thus rid of his human qualities, the sovereign becomes like Heaven. Replicating the cosmic movement, he can then serve as mediator between Heaven and humanity—between nature and society—and make nature's rhythm circulate within the social body.

The organization of space is an act of sovereignty. Like all acts of sovereignty, it involves recourse to force. Violence, even the violence of the State ensuring peace and order to its subjects, can be legitimate only if it is mastered and controlled. Canon II, "The Great Canonical Rules," insists that recourse to weapons is necessary in the exercise of sovereignty, since one of the Yellow Emperor's advisors says, "Even if conflicts are disastrous, if you refuse to fight you will never achieve anything." But canon III, "Aphorisms," provides lessons on moderation, in the form of maxims, sayings, and proverbs, allowing one to guard against excess and to temper the use of force, to somehow control violence and to impose upon it the safeguard of wisdom. Nevertheless, these rules of conduct are only the ethical counterpart of the strategic principle that holds that in order to rule, far from demonstrating one's power, one must be humble and flexible, an idea that runs as an undercurrent throughout *The Four Canons* but is developed especially in two sections, "The Attitude of the Hen and the Rooster" and "The Way of Submission." A few lines chosen at random demonstrate this: "The Way consists of undertaking nothing but being content with responding"; "The sage does not take the initiative, he does not decide by himself, he does not hatch plans, he does not try to seize the advantage; he does not reject gifts from Heaven. He conforms to the order of things"; "The art of facing reversals in one's situation: diminish instead of growing, retreat rather than advancing."

The way in which power was both conceived of and exercised in China during the Warring States Period relied on representations of the cosmic Principle that governs the universe, the Tao. The characteristics that were attributed to the Tao shaped the conception of sovereignty as well as the practice of power throughout China's history. Inversely, the unified, absolutist system that was gradually established at the end of the Warring States Period provides a kind of reflection and model of the functioning of the Principle: that system is only the Principle's expression in the human social sphere. This is why it is essential to study the *Lao Tzu* to understand how the Chinese state functions and to read *The Four Canons* to better discern, through the practice of the Way of good government, how things function as orchestrated by the Tao.

Notes on the Translation from the Chinese

The Four Canons are written in rhythmic, cryptic, intentionally hermetic prose, and I have done my best to render their incantatory quality. With regard to the *Tao Te Ching*, there again I have tried to convey something of the spell its poetic rhythms cast. Of course my translation does not pretend to exhaust the meaning of the text, which operates on many levels simultaneously. The original continually presents a multitude of facets, while the translation can only provide the reflection of a single one, as Borges's essay on the translations of Homer magnificently demonstrates.*

Because the singular work opens in infinite directions, other solutions are always possible, other choices conceivable. Since this presentation immediately falls under the aegis of the relationship between One and many, we can imagine the relationship between original and translation as belonging to the species of relationship between the unicity of the Tao and the multiplicity of manifested beings. The One is one as undifferentiated virtuality and supports all existence, but it is infinite in its concrete manifestations. Similarly, it is immutable and eternal as compared to realized objects subject to the law of change. I would like to offer two examples of how the polysemic elasticity of the language of the original text is inevitably reduced into a univocality of signification in the target language, drawn from sections 38 and 1 of the *Tao Te Ching*. They are better illustrations than a long discussion of the difficulties of the translator's task.

Section 1, appearing at the beginning of the *Book of the Way,* is undoubtedly the most difficult in the entire *Tao Te Ching,* and the first two verses, translated into French as *La voie qui a void n'est pas la vary Voie; le nom qui a nom n'est pas le vary Nom* (literally, "The way that has voice is not the true Way; the name that has name is not the true Name"),

---

*[Jorge Luis Borges. "Some Versions of Homer." *PMLA* 107, no. 5 (Oct. 1992): 1134–38. —*Ed.*]

are the most enigmatic in this section. The Chinese lines *Tao k'o tao (yeh) fei hang tao (yeh), ming k'o ming (yeh) fei heng ming (yeh)*—those final particles *(yeh)* are omitted in the standard versions—lend themselves to all kinds of interpretations, according to the way in which the text is divided and to the meaning given to the word *tao*. That word covers a very wide semantic field in classical Chinese. It indicates the final Principle, the movement of bodies, ways of doing things or techniques—practices, in a word—as well as doctrines, discourse, and the art of political manipulation; moreover, since Chinese does not use morphological marks to distinguish between nouns and verbs, it can mean "to make its way" as well as "way," "to practice" as well as "practice," "to speak" as well as "word." Thus in the phrase in question, a first interpretation, giving the second *tao* the same meaning of "way" as the first but functioning as a verb, would go like this: "The way *(tao)* that can be followed or applied *(tao)* is not a constant way." That is, in actual, real life, we must know how to adapt to circumstances and seize the opportunity of the moment, without ever stiffening into a rigid stance. This is the interpretation given by both strategists and legalists. Moreover, it determines Duyvendak's translation.*

But superimposed over this first interpretation is a second one in which the two *tao*s take different meanings: the first *tao* is taken in the sense of "Way"—that is, the immanent and transcendent Principle from which action draws its origin—and the second in the sense of "speech," of "to say." The meaning of the phrase would then be: "The way that

*[Duyvendak, J. J. L. *Tao Te King: The Book of the Way and Its Virtue*. London: John Murray, 1954. —*Ed.*]

is expressed in words is not the constant Way." All speech, because it is speech, can achieve only particular and partial aspects of reality, which it can never fully reconstruct. A rule for action can be found in no discourse, no doctrine, because in the final Principle there is something that eludes any determination. That is the standard reading. Far from being mutually exclusive, these two meanings complement one another. Indeed, the eternal Tao is found in action and through action, action that is always changing, fluctuating according to the demands of the moment. It is also possible to give the two *taos* the same meaning, this time not of "way" and "to follow the way," but of "discourse" and "to discourse," thus making the two sentences of the passage closely parallel and synonymous. The second chapter of the *Chuang Tzu,* "Discourse on the Identity of Things," adopts this interpretation in the following sequence: "Whoever knows eloquence without words and discourse without speech (*pu yen chih pien, pu tao chih tao*), whoever truly knows them achieves the treasure of Heaven."

Finally, and most recently, beginning from the Mawangdui version in which the two parts of the phrase are punctuated with the particle *ye,* modern scholars propose yet another reading, thanks to a different division: *Tao, k'o tao yeh, fei heng tao yeh.* The meaning would thus be: "The Tao, it can be said (*k'o tao yeh*), but only in a way that is not the one of ordinary discourse (*fei heng tao yeh*)." Thus these lines that open the *Book of the Way* provide justification for the work that is a discourse on the Tao by putting the reader on guard: how to use ordinary language to speak of an entity that exceeds all but heuristic discourse?

In section 38, in the sequence rendered in French as *La Vertu suprême ignore la vertu, c'est pourquoi elle a des versus. La Vertu inférieure s'évertue, c'est pourquoi elle est sans versus* ("Supreme Virtue does not know virtue, that is why it has virtues. Inferior virtue does its best, that is why it is without virtues"), there is continual play between the notions of "reward," "power," "gratitude," and "duty." Interpretation is prompted on the one hand by the breadth of the semantic field of the term *te,* "virtue," meaning efficiency, but also moral virtue and generosity and gratitude arising from meritorious acts of virtue, and on the other hand by the homophony between "virtue," *te,* and the character *te,* "gift," "gain," "success," "result." True virtue, the one of power or potentiality, does not need to be manifested as intentional or conscious action to produce an effect and win the gratitude of others through the benefits it provides to them. Calling it "invisible virtue," Chuang Tzu describes Supreme Virtue as follows: "Water level consists [of] a cavity containing a liquid. The water conserved there without spilling out can serve to measure and indicate the level. The same is true for virtue. Virtue is the expression of the harmony and fulfillment of the self. The one in whom virtue is not manifested in any visible way can come into conflict with no other creature."

In the process of the dissipation of creative efficiency, described in the lines "After the loss of the Tao comes Virtue, after the loss of Virtue comes Goodness, after the loss of Goodness comes Justice . . . ," in addition to its polysemic elasticity, the homophony of the word *te,* "virtue" and *te,* "gain," is amply evoked due to the Chinese postulate by which homophony amounts to synonymy. The decline is activated by the *te,* "virtue," that power emanating from the Tao, which is *te,* "gifts offered as well as taken from another," and thus "acquisition, gain," *te,* of "authority or of power," *te,* since it imposes the duty of "gratitude," *te.* This obligation of the return gift, known by the name of *pao,* the moral imperative of reciprocity, is the source of violence, whether it is the creditor, demanding his due and resorting to force to obtain it, or the debtor, unable to settle his debt and finding himself forced to eliminate the cause of his enslavement. In fact, the duty of reciprocity, which amounts to a categorical imperative, makes vengeance one of the basic obligations of filial piety. Thus the extreme brutality of the line that ends this sequence: "[It] rolls up its sleeves and pummels."

All these ideas are closely connected; they correspond to one another and come together to form a critical evocation of the hierarchizing power of the sacrificial system that establishes the social order through the chain of offerings distributed from the heights of the State to the lowest levels of society in ever wider circles, even while disguising the actual process of the appropriation of wealth, which ascends from the base toward the top. The underlying ideological implications that surface in the terminology borrowed from the categories of formal ritualism are absent in the translation and remain completely inaccessible to the non-Chinese reader. In addition, there is the extraordinary concision of a language in which the repetition in the same sentence of a word with different meanings and functions confers admirable powers of suggestion; the meaning, rhythm, and resonances are gathered into aphorisms, the unyielding density of which renders the core impenetrable.

I usually limit critical apparatus as much as possible

because I remain convinced that notes impede the reading more than they facilitate it. Nevertheless, in the case of *The Four Canons,* we are dealing with a corrupt text, already difficult, and subject to various, even contradictory, interpretations. It seems necessary to provide information essential for understanding the text, and to note other ways of interpreting certain passages when the case presents itself. For the *Tao Te Ching,* I have noted interesting variants and provided clarification on certain essential points.

In the Mawangdui manuscript, *The Four Canons* precedes the *Tao Te Ching;* I have adopted the reverse order in the present translation because it seems to me that reading the *Tao Te Ching* first may clarify many sequences that would otherwise remain obscure to an uninformed reader, thus avoiding misunderstandings of the deep meaning of *The Four Canons* text.*

To produce the translation, I used essentially the following works:

With regard to *The Four Canons:*

• The transcription of the text of *The Four Canons* into simplified characters by the research team for the Mawangdui manuscripts provided by the journal *Wenwu:* "Changsha Mawangdui Hamnu chutu Laozi Yi ben juan qian yishu shiwen." *Wenwu* 10 (1974): 30–42.

---

*[Jean Levi has, however, retained the unusual, reversed order of the two books of the *Tao Te Ching* found in the Mawangdui manuscript. In the interest of clarity, the numbers of the sections remain as they have been assigned in standard editions; thus, in this volume, the *Book of Virtue* (appearing first) is composed of sections 38 to 81; the *Book of the Way* (appearing second) is composed of sections numbered 1 to 37. —*Ed.*]

- The reproduced text, retranscribed into nonsimplified characters and annotated by the research team for the Mawangdui manuscripts, published in 1980, in the first volume of the complete retranscription of the texts and documents discovered in Mawangdui: *Mawangdui Hanmu boshu,* vol. 1.

In addition, I consulted annotated translations into modern Chinese that provided the original text:

- Yu Mingguang. *Huangdi sijing jinzhu jinyi.* Changsha: Yuelu shushe, 1993.
- Gu Bin and Zhang Huishu. *Huangdi sijing zhu yi.* Beijing: Zhongguo shehui kexue chubanshe, 2004.

as well as annotated English translations that provided the original text:

- Robin D. S. Yates. *Five Lost Classics: Tao, Huang-Lao, and Yin-Yang in Han China.* New York: Ballantine Books, 1997.
- Leo S. Chang and Yu Feng. *The Four Political Treatises of the Yellow Emperor.* Honolulu: University of Hawaii Press, 1998.

There is a French translation of *The Four Canons* by Jacques Decaux (*Les Quatre Livres de l'empereur Jaune. Le canon taoïque retrouvé.* Taipei: Ouyu chubanshe, 1989), but it was impossible for me to acquire it; similarly, I could not get hold of the annotated translation into modern Chinese by

Chen Guying (*Huangdi sijing jinzhu jinyi, Mawangdui Hanmu chutu boshu*. Taipei: Taiwan Shangwu yinshuguan, 1995) because of the impoverished state of French university libraries. I myself, incidentally, have published extracts from *The Four Canons* in a collection of political texts of the Warring States titled *Dangers du discours* (Aix: Alinéa, 1985).

With regard to the *Tao Te Ching*, my translation was based on:

- The transcription into simplified characters by the research team for the Mawangdui manuscripts published in Beijing in 1976 by Wenwu chubanshe (Cultural Relics Publishing House).
- The reproduced text, retranscribed into nonsimplified characters and annotated by the Mawangdui research team, published in 1980 in the first volume of the complete transcription of all the texts and documents discovered in Mawangdui: *Mawandgui Hanmu boshu,* vol. 1.

In addition, for the standard text I consulted:

- The version with comments by Wang Bi in *Wang Bi ji jiaoshi*. Beijing: Zhongua shuju, 1:1–192.
- The *Laozi Benyi* by Wei Yuan, in *Zhuzi jicheng,* vol. 3. Beijing: Zhonghua shuju, 1986.
- The English translation by Arthur Waley. *The Way and its Power.* London: George Allen and Unwin, 1968 (first edition 1934).
- The English translation by D. C. Lau. *Lao Tzu, Tao*

Te Ching. London: Penguin Books, 1976 (first edition 1963).

- The French translation by Liou Kia-hway. *Lao-tseu,* in *Philosophes taoïstes I.* Paris: Gallimard, 1980 (first edition 1967).
- The French translation by François Houang and Pierre Leyris. *La Voie et sa Vertu.* Paris: Le Seuil, 1979 (revised edition, first edition 1949).

I also looked at the Guodian *Laozi,* the manuscript of which was published and retranscribed in the volume where all the texts on bamboo strips exhumed at Guodian appear, titled *Guodian Chuma zhujian.* Beijing: Wenwu chubanshe, 1998.

Finally, a translation based on three versions of Wang Pi and the Guodian and Mawangdui manuscripts, by Rémi Mathieu, was published just recently by Entrelacs éditions, in March 2008, called *Le Daode jing. Classique de le Voie et de son efficace*; I was not able to consult it for my own translation, which I had completed by this date.

The transcription system I have adopted is that of the École française d'Extrême-Orient, most agreeable to the French reader's eye, with the exception of bibliographical references, provided in the pinyin transcription system now most commonly used in academic circles.

Altered or omitted passages are indicated with ellipses in brackets: [. . .]; when a word, part of a phrase, a whole phrase, or even a passage appears in brackets, it indicates a conjectural reconstruction of that text.

TAO TE CHING
THE BOOK OF THE WAY
AND OF VIRTUE

This version preserves the unusual, reversed order of the two books of the *Tao Te Ching* in the Mawangdui manuscript. In the interest of clarity, the numbers of the sections remain as they have been assigned in standard editions; thus, in this volume, the *Book of Virtue* (appearing first) is composed of sections 38 to 81; the *Book of the Way* (appearing second) is composed of sections numbered 1 to 37.

THE BOOK OF VIRTUE

Supreme Virtue does not know virtue,
that is why it has virtues.
Inferior virtue does its best,
that is why it is without virtues.
Supreme Virtue neither acts nor wants,
supreme Goodness acts but does not want,
supreme Justice* acts and wants,
supreme Ritual acts and, lacking response,
rolls up its sleeves and pummels.
That is why it is said:
"After the loss of the Tao comes Virtue,
after the loss of Virtue comes Goodness,
after the loss of Goodness comes Justice,
after the loss of Justice comes Ritual."
Ritual is the husk of faith
and the source of disorder.
Foresight is an outgrowth of the Tao;
it is the outer room of foolishness.

---

*The manuscript has the word *te*, "virtue," for *yi*, "justice," a transcription error.

The sage considers the heart not the husk,
He holds the fruit not the outgrowth.
He rejects that one, takes this one.* (38)

These are the ones who once obtained the One:
thanks to the One, Heaven was clear,
the Earth stable,
the gods sacred,
the valleys filled,†
the princes ruled the empire.
At which point it could be said:
if it was not clear Heaven would crack,
not stable, the Earth would collapse,
not sacred, the gods would die,
not full, the valleys would dry up,
not eminent, the princes would fall.
The noble has the base for foundation,
the high has the low for basis.
Sovereigns call themselves
"orphan," "widow," "disconsolate":
could they be aware of their humble roots?
True renown is without renown;
do not try to ring like jade
or to sound like resonant stones. (39)

Return is the Tao's movement,
weakness its action.

---

*"That one" and "this one" here indicate the external and the internal.
†The phrase "the beings engendered" that follows "the valleys filled" in standard versions is omitted.

The ten thousand beings are born of being,
being is born of nothingness. (40)

When the good man hears word of the Way,
he hurries to put it into practice.
When the average man hears word of the Way,
he takes from it what he wants to hear.
When the worthless man hears word of the Way,
he makes fun of it.
It would no longer be the Way if he did not
    laugh at it.
That is what these maxims express:
"The bright way is dark,
the way that progresses recedes,
the smooth way is rough,
the highest virtue is like a ravine,
true candor seems sullied,
the amplest virtue narrow,
the firmest virtue shaky,
absolute sincerity seems suspicious.
A great square has no corners,
a great vase takes long to perfect,
great music spares notes,
the great image has no form,
the Tao is too great to have a name,
the one that completes all it undertakes."* (41)

---

*The standard version includes "The hidden and nameless Tao supports and
accomplishes."

The Tao gives birth to the One,
the One to the Two, the Two to the Three;
from the Three are born the ten thousand
      beings.
The ten thousand beings, back to yin, front to
      yang,
united in the primordial breath
to produce harmony.
Men detest nothing more   ·
than being orphaned, widowed, disconsolate:
those are the titles that kings pride themselves on.
Thus things grow to be diminished
and diminished, grow.
What others teach,
I note and teach in turn:
if I knew a violent man who did not come to a
      sad end,
I would choose him as my mentor. (42)

Do you not see that in this world the supplest
straddles the stiffest?
Nothingness seeps into what has no gaps;
thus revealing the advantages of non-action.
But few in the empire have access   .
to the mute lesson that would initiate them. (43)

Which do you cherish more, your reputation or
      your body?
Which do you value more, your goods or your
      being?

Which upsets you more, to lose or to acquire?
That is why the one who balks at the expense
   squanders,
who amasses too much sustains heavy losses,
who knows to be content suffers no offense,
who knows when to stop avoids perils,
and enjoys long life. (44)

A beautiful object seems chipped,
but using it cannot wear it out.
A full spring seems empty,
but it is never exhausted.
Great straightness seems curved,
great skill seems clumsy,
a great victory is just like a defeat,
activity remedies a chill,
rest, a fever.
Be pure, be calm,
you will rectify the universe.* (45)

---

*The manuscript is very corrupt here, so that only eleven characters remain legible. We are completing it according to version A of the Mawangdui *Lao Tzu,* as the intact characters of manuscript B correspond closely to those of the manuscript A version. In this version, as in the Guodian manuscript on bamboo strips, the phrase "a great victory is just like a defeat" appears in the place of "great eloquence stammers," as in standard versions. Nevertheless, are we looking at the original teaching here? In chapter 2 of the *Chuang Tzu,* we find these paradoxical expressions that seem reminiscent of this section: "The Tao has no name, eloquence does without words, goodness is not charitable, integrity is not inflexible, valor is not violent"; this would lead us to believe that phrases like "a great eloquence stammers" could appear in certain versions earlier than the Mawangdui ones.

When the empire follows the Way,
the chargers manure the fields.
When the empire has lost it,
the war horses foal in the workers' districts.
I know no greater price
than being unsatisfied.
I know no worse hardship
than being insatiable,
no misfortune more painful
than the lure of gain.
The one who considers himself content
will always have his fill. (46)

Without leaving our doorstep,
we know the world.
Without looking out the window,
we see into the movements of Heaven.
The farther you go,
the less you know.
The sage knows without traveling,
penetrates without peering,
works without acting.* (47)

---

*The theoretician of imperial absolutism, Han Fei (third century BCE), gives an excellent interpretation of this passage in his commentary on the *Tao Te Ching*: "The orifices are the doors of understanding; sounds and colors dull sight and hearing; the mind exhausts itself contemplating external forms; that is how we lose our guiding center. We are incapable of noticing misfortunes, even if they are as big as mountains. That is why the *Lao Tzu* says, 'Without leaving one's door,' and so on. The mind must never leave the fullness of its dwelling place." For Han Fei, the maxim has political implications: to govern, the sovereign must never make use of his senses or his intelligence but rely completely on those infallible instruments, the laws and ordinances.

Whoever devotes himself to study grows day
    after day,
Whoever instructs himself in the Tao diminishes
    day after day.
He diminishes and diminishes until there is
    nothing left to do.
Whoever does nothing can do everything.
Do you want to make off with the universe? Be
    idle.
The busy are unfit to win the empire. (48)

The sage has no ideas.
Everyone's ideas are his ideas.
What is good, he finds good,
what is not good, he finds good, too,
that is why everything is good to him.
What is worthy of faith, he has faith in,
what is not, he puts faith in, too,
and that is why he earns confidence.
The sage is on his guard in society,
because he knows how to keep from the outer
    world
the divine confusion he harbors in his heart.
Most of us are enslaved by our eyes and ears,
while he laughs at them, blissful as a babe. (49)

We exit into life,
we enter into death.
Thirteen steadfast in life,

thirteen steadfast in death.
Thirteen in life,
the mortal grounds of movement.
Why? Because we live life too quickly.
Whoever knows how to nurture his life
encounters no rhinoceroses or tigers
in his travels.
He will have to bear no weapons or armor
when he enters armies.
The rhinoceros does not know where to gore him,
the tiger where to lodge its claw,
the spear where to thrust its point.
Why? He is not of mortal ground. (50)

The Tao gives them life,
its Virtue nurtures them,
forming them into beings
or fashioning them into objects.
That is why creatures
revere the Tao and honor its Virtue,
without any title to ensure majesty
possessed for all eternity.*

---

*The manuscript offers the reading of *chüeh,* meaning first "goblet of alcohol," and by extension, "title of nobility," in the place of *ming,* as in the standard versions, understood by commentators to mean here "order," or "command"; hence the usual translation of "not dictated (*ming*) by duty but by natural inclination." But *ming* can also mean "to enthrone a charge," "to entrust a mandate," as in the first paragraph of the second chapter of *The Four Canons of the Yellow Emperor.* And that is the meaning that must be understood here, as the Mawangdui text clearly shows: the Tao and Virtue are noble by nature; otherwise, this nobility would need to be supported with a title or enthronement, exterior to its intrinsic being.

The Tao gives them life and nurtures them,
it makes them grow, raises them, coddles them,
sustains them, feeds them, protects them.
Giving life without demands,
producing without taking pride in it,
promoting growth without taking charge,
is that not mysterious Virtue? (51)

The world has an origin:
I call it the Mother of the Tao.
Whoever grasps the mother knows the son,
whoever knows the son will know how to guard
 the mother
and will always be sheltered from misfortune.
Block your orifices,
close all your doors,
your life will never be exhausted.
Open your orifices,
multiply activities,
and your life is without recourse.
Whoever sees the small, I call penetrating.
Confining yourself to weakness, that is strength.
Using your radiance
to make the light return
by being careful not to attract misfortune,
that is following the natural law. (52)

If I had an ounce of wisdom,
when I am on the main road,

my great fear would be deviating from it.
The great Way is smooth,
but the crowd likes shortcuts.
The palaces are well polished,
but the fields badly tended
and the granaries empty.
They don rich attire,
and sharp swords.
They stuff themselves and get drunk,
having more than they need:
it is the ship of thieves
that does not know the Way. (53)

What is well planted does not let itself be
    destroyed,
what is well grasped does not let itself be robbed.
The ancient worship is transmitted from father
    to son.
Applied to one's body, Virtue is uprightness,
cultivated in the family, Virtue is abundant,
cultivated in a province, Virtue is proliferating,
cultivated in a country, Virtue is burgeoning,
cultivated in the empire, Virtue is encompassing.
Know the body through the body,
the family through the family,
the province through the province,
the country the country,
the empire through the empire.
How do I know the empire is that way?
Through this. (54)

Whoever possesses the vital force
is like the newborn,
spared by venomous beasts,
ferocious animals,
as well as birds of prey.
His bones are supple,
his tendons flexible,
and his grip powerful.
He knows nothing of sex,
but his penis is erect
because his vitality is at its height.
He wails all day long without getting hoarse,
his harmony being perfect.
To know harmony is called constancy.
To know constancy is called illumination.
To love life too much does not bode well.
The mind does violence to the breath in wanting
　　to control it.
Old age follows the fullness of power.
All that runs counter to the Tao.
What runs counter to the Tao knows an early
　　end. (55)

Whoever knows does not speak.
Whoever speaks does not know.
Obstruct every opening,
close every door,
merge all light,
unite all dust,

dull all that cuts,
unravel all the knots.
Such is dark identity.
You can
neither approach it nor keep it at a distance,
neither benefit nor harm it,
neither honor nor demean it,
that is why it is revered throughout the empire. (56)

A State is governed through regular means,
a war is conducted through irregular means,
but it is through doing nothing
that one seizes the universe.
How do I know this is so?
The more taboos and prohibitions rule,
the poorer the people become.
The more one relies on good tools,
the more disorder rages.
The more ingenious minds there are,
the more frivolous luxury develops.
The more ordinances multiply,*
the more the bandits swarm.
That is why the sage says:

---

*The manuscript text is defective and only the word *wu* (thing) can be read
in the place of *ling* (ordinance) as in the standard version; but the Guodian
manuscript contains the complete reading *fa-wu,* which signifies "beautiful
objects." So there is little doubt that the Mawangdui text must also use the
same expression. Thus the sentence may mean, as some modern scholars
believe, "The more beautiful objects are made, the more thieves rampage."
This idea is developed further in section 3 (". . . do not seek rare goods if
you do not want [the people] to be thieves, do not display desirable objects

"I do nothing
and the people improve.
I remain silent
and the people govern themselves.
I undertake nothing
and the people grow rich.
I desire to be without desires,
and the people rediscover simplicity." (57)

Under an indulgent master, the people
    are pure,
under an irksome regime, underhanded.
Misfortune is the source of happiness,
happiness turns back into misfortune,
who knows for how long?
Since there is no stable form,
what is normal turns into its opposite,
the beneficial into the malevolent.
Human distraction is old as the hills.
The sage is forthright without being curt,
honest without being disdainful,
straightforward without being abrupt,
luminous without being blinding. (58)

---

if you do not want to trouble their hearts." The substitution of the word *ling* for the word *wu* may have taken place when the meaning of *fa* in the sense of "beautiful," "perfect," would no longer have been understood (as it took on its current meaning of "law"). Nevertheless, the word *wu* does not mean only "object," "thing," but also "business," "activity," "task," "function." And thus the expression *fa-wu* could just as easily have the meaning of "police operations" and be more or less equivalent to *fa-ling*.

To rule humanity and serve nature
there is nothing like economy.
Economy: means of early submission.
Through it I accumulate a double share of Virtue.
Whoever has a double reserve of Virtue
will dominate all.
Dominating all, who knows one's limits?
Whoever knows no limits
is master of the realm;
whoever possesses the Mother of the realm
can enjoy it a long time.
That is what I call
sinking in one's roots,
strengthening the rootstock.
Such is the Way of long life
and of eternal vision. (59)

Running a great State
is like frying a small fish.
If the Tao watches over the world,
the demons lose their power.
Not only do the demons lose their power,
but that power no longer torments men.
Not only does that power no longer torment men,
but the sages themselves no longer torment men.
They no longer harm one another.
Virtue is exchanged and returns. (60)

A great nation
is the lower course of a river,

the meeting point of the universe,
the female of creation.
The female, through her passivity,
will always get the better of the male.
To be passive is to humble oneself.
A large country humbles itself before a small one
to enlist it;
a small country humbles itself before a large one
so that it enlists it.
One humbles itself and takes,
the other humbles itself and gives.
The first needs to expand its circle of regulars,
the second to enter the service of a great power.
But for them both to obtain what they desire,
the greater one must bow. (61)

My Way is the point of attraction of the
          universe.*
It is the treasure of the good man
and the safeguard of the good-for-nothing.
Fine words buy titles,
fine deeds place you above the crowd.

---

*The standard versions have the word *ao,* which literally means "the south-west corner of the house where seed is stored to protect it from the sun," and by extension implies "hidden," "secret." In its place the two Mawangdui manuscripts have the word *chu,* "to flow," "to draw attention," the term used in section 49 to describe the action of the external world upon most people whose eyes and ears are fascinated by the variety of phenomena. Thus there is some irony here regarding the simultaneously parallel and opposite effects of the external world and the Way.

So what good is it to rail against the baseness of
    others?
For the accession of a king, the nomination of a
    minister,
instead of offering horse-drawn chariots and
    great pomp,
would it not be better to make them the gift of
    the Way?
Why was it esteemed by the Ancients?
Not because it was said of it:
"It allows you to escape punishment"?
That is why it is so prized by the empire. (62)

Practice non-action,
let go the letting go,
savor the tasteless,
magnify the tiny,
attach great importance to little,
respond to hatred with gifts,
prevent difficulty with ease,
through small acts produce great effects.
Not working on a large scale,
the sage's successes are large.
Whoever makes promises lightly
is not worthy of trust.
Whoever finds everything easy
runs into the worst difficulties.
Finding everything difficult
the sage never encounters obstacles. (63)

What is at rest is easy to maintain,
what has yet to transpire is easy to prevent,
what is brittle is easy to break,
what is wispy is easy to disperse.
Act on what is not yet,
Rule what is not unruly.
That tree that fills both arms
was born from a tiny seed.
That nine-story tower
rose from a lump of earth.
A thousand-league journey
begins with a single step.
Whoever acts will fail,
whoever clings will lose:
the sage does not fail since he does not act,
he does not lose since he does not cling.
When managing their affairs,
people fail right at the end.
Whoever is vigilant at the end as at the
        beginning
will succeed in his undertakings.
The sage desires not to desire,
he does not value what is difficult to acquire;
he learns to unlearn,
returning along the path that the crowd rejects;
and, adhering to the spontaneity of beings,
he does nothing. (64)

Those who used to possess the Way
did not use it to enlighten the people
but to make them dimmer.
What makes people rebellious
is excessive cleverness.
Whoever governs a country through reason
commits a crime against it;
whoever governs it without bright ideas
is its benefactor.
Keeping this opposition ever in mind
is the standard and the compass on which to
        model oneself.
Always knowing the standard and the compass
is to possess mysterious Virtue.
Mysterious Virtue plunges deep and extends far,
it accompanies things on their return
and achieves great conformity. (65)

If the rivers and seas rule over the streams,
that is because they are the lower ones.
That is how they rule over the streams.
The sage humbles himself in words in order to rise.
He places himself behind to take the lead.
He holds himself above the people without
        weighing them down,
he takes charge without giving offense.
The whole empire promotes him without tiring
        of him:

never contesting, no one dreams of contesting
 anything with him. (66)

The whole world says that my doctrine is great
but that it resembles nothing else.
It is great to resemble nothing else.
If it resembled something,
it would have been nothing for a long time now!
I have three treasures that I guard.
The first is love,
the second is parsimony,
the third, "I-do-not-dare-to-be-first."
Loving, I will be brave,
parsimonious, I will be generous,
not daring to be first,
I will take the lead in matters.
Whoever is brave without love,
is generous without parsimony,
takes the lead without putting himself last,
is headed for ruin.
Through love, the offensive agent
draws support from the defensive,
Heaven assists you
and protects you by its love. (67)

Whoever has the stuff of an officer is not
 soldierly,
the great warrior has no rage for killing.
You defeat the enemy without an encounter,
you command by humbling yourself.

That is what is called non-violence,
that is what is called manipulation,
that is what is called matching Heaven.
Such was ancient perfection. (68)

This saying is popular among the strategists:
"Be attacked rather than attacking;
retreat a foot rather than advancing an inch."
That is what is called
deployment without preemptive strike,
rolling up one's sleeves without any arms,
drawing one's weapons without facing a threat,
charging a nonexistent enemy.
There is no misfortune greater than having no
    enemy.*
Whoever has no enemy risks losing his treasures.
When two armies of equal force confront each
    other,
the most tearful one wins. (69)

My doctrine is easy to understand and to
    practice,
nevertheless no one understands or practices it.
All speech has a source, all action has a subject.
Not knowing them, the crowd does not know
    me.

---

*Standard versions all say, "There is no misfortune greater than despising the enemy," which is less strong and, more importantly, less in keeping with the sequence, in which it is a matter of presenting nothingness to the other, so that, deprived of an adversary, he inflicts defeat upon himself.

Little known, I am precious.*
Sage hiding jade under his homespun robe. (70)

To know what one does not know is excellence;
To believe what one knows without knowing is
   an ill.
To be ill with one's ill
is to get rid of that ill.
The sage is not affected by any ill;
nothing being ill for him,
no ill can make him ill. (71)

When the people no longer fear authority,
it leads to additional authority.
Do not lodge the people in too cramped
   quarters;
keep from squeezing them too hard.
If you refrain from burdening them,
you will not make them detest you.
The sage knows himself but does not display
   himself,
he values himself without praising himself to the
   skies,
thus he rejects that for this. (72)

---

*According to the formulation of the sentence in standard versions, this must be translated, "Rare are those who follow me, noble those who imitate me," but the omission of *chih,* "those who," in the second part of the sentence in the Mawangdui version allows for our reading, by giving the word *tzu,* "to imitate," "to model after," the function of conjunction, "thus," "so that," rather than verb, and by linking the sentence to the following one, which is incongruous otherwise.

Whoever has the courage to dare gets himself
    killed,
whoever has the courage not to dare remains
    alive.
Of these two behaviors
one benefits and the other harms.
Who knows the reason
for Heaven's hatreds?
Heaven possesses the art
of conquering without fighting,
getting answers without speaking,
summoning without calling,
making plans without trying.
Heaven's net is immense,
letting nothing escape
its open mesh. (73)

If the people do not fear death,
what good is it to threaten them with the law's
    wrath?
Even supposing it haunted them
and I succeeded in laying hold of the offenders,
to put them to death properly,
who would dare to carry it out?
For the people to tremble,
an executioner must always stand ready.
But who will act in his place,
knowing that taking up the ax

in the great carpenter's stead
entails great risk of losing a hand? (74)

If the people are starving,
it is because the taxes of the rich
take bread from their mouths.
That is why the people are hungry!
If the people are unruly
it is because the rulers who govern them
give them no rest.
That is why they are unruly!
If the people have no concern for death,
it is because the nobles are too busy
    living well.
That is why they have no concern for death!
Not living to live is wiser
than paying the price of living well. (75)

Man is born supple and soft
and dies hard and rigid;
Tender and flexible at birth, the trees,
once dead, are dry and brittle.
That is why it is said:
"The hard and rigid are the patrons of death,
the tender and flexible, the patrons of life."
Too powerful an army will not be able to win,
the strongest trees are the first to be broken.
The strong and hard are always below,
the supple and weak always above. (76)

Heaven is an archer flexing his bow:
it equalizes high and low
supplements the shortage, trims the excess.
It takes the surplus, fills the gap.
As for man, he takes from the one who has
    nothing
to give to the one who has everything.
Who would distribute his surpluses to the empire
if not the one who possesses the Way?
The sage acts without expecting anything,
accomplishes without taking pride in his works,
because he has no interest in flaunting his gifts. (77)

There is nothing more fluid and weak than water,
but for wearing down what is hard and strong,
nothing surpasses it, nothing can replace it.
That water defeats the hard as weak defeats
    strong:
no one in the empire does not know this
but no one draws a lesson from it.
It is a wise saying that goes:
"Whoever accepts the refuse of a realm
is the master of its ancestral altars.
Whoever takes upon himself a country's
    calamities
is called the king of the universe."
The truest sayings seem the most false. (78)

Even pacified, if the aftereffects of rancor remain,
can it be called good?

Holding acknowledgments of debts,
the sage refrains from claiming his due.
The virtuous man is the Keeper of the Seals,
the man without virtue, the Taxation Officer.
Heaven gives to good men, unbiased. (79)

I imagine a small, scarcely populated country,
where if there had been tools
to increase productivity a hundredfold,
everyone would have refused to use them.*
A country where you would hate to die far from
    home;
where, even if there were barges and carts,
no one would have known what to fill them with.
A country where, if there were weapons,
no one would have had any reason to brandish
    them,

---

*Most commentators understand the expression *shan-po chih ch'i,* "instruments for ten or one hundred," as a circumlocution for weapons, the population being divided into troops of ten and one hundred when it went into battle. But Arthur Waley's interpretation seems preferable to me; the expression must indeed be compared to one appearing in the *Shang-chün shou,* where the detractor of the legalist Shang Yang's reforms says that the laws must not be modified unless advantages would multiply a hundred times or tools altered unless productivity would increase tenfold. The Mawangdui text with the expression *shih pai jen ch'i,* "instruments [worth] ten or a hundred men," seems to confirm Waley's intuition. The idea that technical innovations and mechanical inventions are fundamentally bad, because they mechanize the heart even if they reduce human labor, is an essential theme in ancient Taoism. It informs a famous dialogue in the *Chuang Tzu* between an old gardener and a disciple of Confucius. Moreover, if it were a matter of weapons, the phrase would be redundant with what follows.

where, for writing,
they would have stuck to knotting cords.
A country where they would have been satisfied
     with their food
and content with their clothes;
where they would take pleasure in their customs
and prove happy in their fate.*
A country where, though the neighboring region
     was so close
you could see its people
and hear their roosters and dogs answering
     yours,
you would die of old age
having never visited there. (80)

Sincere words are not beautiful,
beautiful words are not sincere.
Wisdom is not erudition,
erudition is not wisdom.
Quality is not quantity,
quantity is not quality.

---

*In most standard versions, the phrase translated here as "and prove happy in their fate" comes before "would take pleasure in their customs" and thus takes a different, more concrete meaning, since it follows food and clothing and must thus be rendered by "would appear content with their abodes." Some versions, the "Fuyi" version for example, have in place of *an ch'i chü,* "would prove content with their lot," the expression *le ch'i ye,* "would be delighted with their occupations," which has an equivalent meaning. The *Chuang Tzu,* which echoes that description word-for-word in a diatribe against civilization and sages who promoted it, repeats the Mawangdui version.

The sage does not accumulate:
the more he sacrifices, the more he has,
the more he gives, the richer he is.
Heaven's role consists of being beneficial and not
    harmful,
man's role must be to strive and not to compete.
    (81)

THE BOOK OF THE WAY

The way given voice is not the true Way.
The name with a name is not the true Name.
The Nameless, origin of Heaven and Earth,
the Named, mother of the ten thousand beings.
In the absence of all desire,
one contemplates its mystery.
Through the presence of desire,
one contemplates what it bounds.
Two aspects of a single thing,
two synonymous designations*
Mystery of mysteries,
gateway of wonders. (1)

It is because everyone recognizes
beauty as beauty that there is ugliness.
It is because everyone knows
what is good that there is bad.

---

*The text of standard versions differs slightly: "Born of a single origin, they
bear different names, but one and the other alike have the same designation
of 'mysterious.'"

Being and Non-Being engender one another,
easy and difficult complete each other,
long and short give each other form,
high and low complement each other,
voice and tones respond to one another,
before and after succeed each other,
that is the norm.
The sage keeps busy doing nothing
and practices teaching without words.
He lets things go and undertakes nothing.
He achieves success without dwelling on it,
and nothing happens since he does not dwell
    on it. (2)

Do not honor the worthy,
and the people will not be quarrelsome;
do not seek rare goods
if you do not want them to be thieves;
do not display desirable objects
if you do not want to trouble their hearts.
That is why the sage, when he governs,
empties their heads
and fills their stomachs.
He weakens their wills
and strengthens their bones.
He banishes from the people all thought, all desire,
and puts all quick minds at his service,
so that all is perfectly ruled. (3)

Oh Tao, flowing spring
to draw from forever inexhaustible,
abyss that seems like the ancestor of things,
you dull all sharp blades,
untangle all knots,
merge all light,
unite all dust,
so deep that you seem almost to exist.
I do not know whose son you are:
you could be the grandfather of God. (4)

Heaven and Earth are inhuman,
they treat beings like straw dogs.
The sage is inhuman,
he treats men like straw dogs.
Between Heaven and Earth,
is it not like a forge's bellows,
empty and inexhaustible.
The more you stoke it, the more it blows.
Wanting to know everything quickly exhausts you:
it is best to occupy the center.* (5)

---

*The two Mawangdui versions have *wen*, "to hear," "to find out," in place of *yen*, "to speak," "to hold forth," which changes the meaning of the passage considerably and gives it a more political, even regulatory, orientation. It is not a question here of discourse on the Tao for which no speech can exhaust the meaning and nature, but of techniques of manipulation and control practiced by the sovereign who, at the center of the realm like the empty hub of a wheel, brings information together thanks to the tight control of populations ensured by the interlocking of the united territories, without which he would need to conduct inquiries by himself. This meaning is developed in the appendix of *The Four Canons of the Yellow Emperor*, in particular in the first paragraph of section 1 of the first canon, "The Law Way."

The Valley spirit never dies,
this is the Dark Female.
The gateway of the Dark Female
is the root of Earth and Heaven.
Infinite silk thread that seems almost to exist,
and that is used without ever exhausting it. (6)

Earth and Heaven are eternal.
They are eternal in not living for themselves.
That is why they exist forever.
The sage keeps to the background and he is
    pushed to the fore.
A stranger to himself, he endures.
Stripped of all egoism,
he realizes his ambitions. (7)

The supreme good is like water:
beneficial to all, water is rival to nothing.
Occupying those low places disdained by all,
it is infinitely close to the Tao.
In dwelling, it is only earthly,
in thought only unfathomable,
in giving only celestial,
in speech only sincere,
in government only well ordered,
in work only efficient,
in movement only timely.
What is rival to nothing is without reproach. (8)

Stop accumulating.
Whatever is too well sharpened gets dull.*
Will you be able to guard from thieves
those rooms full of gold and jade?
The rich man draped with honors
attracts misfortune through his pride.
To withdraw once the work is accomplished
is truly the way of Heaven. (9)

Can your soul embrace the One
and with it form an indivisible whole?
By focusing your breath, can you
recapture the newborn's suppleness?
Can you purify the dark mirror of your soul†

---

*In place of *chih,* "to hold," the text has the homophone *chih,* "to prosper," "to accumulate," "to make fruitful." In the standard as well as the Mawangdui versions, the sentence that follows is not only unintelligible but fits poorly in the sequence; the text should surely be amended according to the Guodian manuscript that includes characters unclear in meaning but that roughly might signify the following: "Filling your granaries too full, you will make your wheat rot," which would be a modulation of the idea articulated through all the concrete examples given afterward, that by amassing too much one risks losing all and that downfall awaits those who rise too high.

†In place of *lan,* "to see," "vision," the manuscript has the word *chien,* which is related in meaning and which is distinguished graphically only by the absence of the radical (semantic component) for "sight." It could thus be read as "to purify your inner vision," as it has been by all translators. But *chien* is often used for the homophone *chien,* "mirror," which is distinguished by the simple addition of the character for metal. Since the expression *chao chien,* "bright mirror," is a cliché, it seems to me that the author was playing with that second meaning of the word by using the antonym *hsüan chien,* "dark mirror," to evoke a movement that runs counter to ordinary experience; hence my translation, which attempts to render the oxymoron.

until all impurity is washed away?
Do you know how to cherish the people and
    nurture a country
without making use of your intelligence?
Opening and closing the doors of Heaven,
do you know how to play the role of the hen?
In the white radiance of illumination,
will you be able to let go of your reason?
Oh you who gives life and nourishes,
you give life without appropriating,
you prompt growth without taking charge,
because such is mysterious Virtue. (10)

The thirty spokes converge at the hub:
emptiness is needed for the wheel to turn.
A vessel is formed out of clay,
emptiness is needed for it to hold water.
Doors and windows are cut into a house,
emptiness is needed for it to provide shelter.
Matter is useful, but its absence
makes a thing function. (11)

Colors dull the view,
flavors ruin the taste,
sounds deafen the ear,
hunting and riding alarm the heart,
priceless objects prompt crime.
The sage, in his government,
attends to the stomach and not the eye.
He dismisses that to privilege this. (12)

"Favor and disfavor merit fear."

"Rank is an ill as great as the body."

What does it mean, "Favor and disfavor merit
    fear"?

Favor erodes: thus winning it prompts fear; but
    losing it does, too.*

That is what I take "Favor and disfavor merit
    fear" to mean.

And what does "Rank is as great an ill as the
    body" mean?

All man's misfortunes come from having a body.

Indeed, what misfortune could befall him if he
    were deprived of it?

Whoever attaches more value to watching over
    his body than the empire

deserves to find it entrusted to him.

Whoever would rather care for himself than the
    empire

is worthy of receiving it in trust. (13)

Looking at it, you do not see it:

it is called the Invisible;

Listening to it, you do not hear it:

it is called the Inaudible.

Touching it, you do not feel it:

it is called the Impalpable.

---

*By dividing the sentence as Wang Pi does, this could also mean: "For a sub-
ject, receiving the favors [of the sovereign] prompts fear . . ."

Three unfathomable states
that are absorbed into the One.
The One, neither blurred at its height,
nor muddled at its base,
so fine it cannot be named,
it returns to no-thing.
Formless form,
image of nothing,
fleeting, ungraspable,
from behind you cannot see its back,
from in front you cannot see its head.
Use today's secrets,*
and you will be master of the present.
To know the dawn of origins
is called the Law of the Tao. (14)

Those who formerly practiced the Way
were subtle, mysterious, unfathomable.
Unfathomable, I can only try to describe their
        appearance:
hesitant as though they were crossing a frozen river,
circumspect as though they feared their neighbors,
solemn as though paying a visit,
they melted like snow in the sun,
and then seemed dazed as stumps,
troubled as muddy water,
gaping as valleys,

---

*The two Mawangdui versions have the word *chin*, "today," instead of *ku*, "in
the past." A transcription error or, in fact, the original meaning?

troubled water that, resting, gradually clears,
resting body that, slowly, movement brings back
    to life.
Whoever devotes himself to that art is not
    seeking fulfillment,
not seeking fulfillment, he is endlessly renewed.* (15)

Achieve emptiness and you will be the axis of
    the world;
preserve your serenity and you will be its
    benchmark.†

---

*This is a description of techniques for adapting the breath that confer the power to regulate the life of the body, thanks to knowledge acquired by listening to it. There is a progression, marked by the passage from a solid state (ice, solemnity) to a liquid state. It is as though the body dissolves, changing from rigid to fluid. This change is even more pronounced in the Mawangdui version where all the characters evoking the stages of the body's transformation (the effect of adapting the latent energies it harbors), beginning from the decisive moment of the ice melting, contain the radical for water, and thus connote fluidity. Even graphically, these characters manifest the Tao's investment in the human body, water being the entity closest to the Way in the domain of forms.
†The two parallel sentences are ordinarily translated as meaning "Attain supreme emptiness and firmly maintain your tranquility"; in giving a nominal sense to the words *ki* and *tou*, the words "emptiness" and "tranquility" become determinants: "summits of emptiness" and "stability of tranquility." The lessons of Mawangdui allow, thanks to the presence of the final particle *ye*, which has the value of a copula, the phrase to be constructed differently and give *ki* and *tou* an attributive function. Furthermore, the texts carry in the second part of the phrase the words *piao*, "marker," "reference point," in manuscript A and *tou*, "inspector," "observer," in manuscript B—amended by the editors of the texts as *tou*, "calm"—and because of their parallel nature there is every reason to give to the word *ki*, meaning "supreme" or "extremity," its full sense of "fixed astronomic reference" and "celestial axis." The passage then takes on a much stronger sense and resonance with *The Four Canons of the Yellow Emperor* and the *Ho-kouan-tseu*.

Facing the multitude of beings,
I contemplate their return.
Creation, an endless carousel,
always returns to its root.
Returning to the root brings serenity,
serenity brings a return to innate nature,
returning to innate nature obeys the norm.
Whoever knows the norm is enlightened,
whoever does not is blinded.
Blindness summons misfortune.
To know the norm is to welcome all;
whoever welcomes all is universal,
whoever is universal is royal,
whoever is royal is Heaven,
whoever is Heaven is the Way,
whoever is the Way will endure
and will always be safe. (16)

Of the best, they know only that he exists,
the little less good they love and praise,
the even less good they fear,
the very worst they scorn.
Not inspiring confidence
will create bad faith.
Wary, the sage weighs each word.
The work brought to completion and his
    task accomplished,
the people declare: "I have decided it
    thus." (17)

When the great Way was abandoned
Goodness and Justice were born;
the appearance of intelligence
was accompanied by artifice.
Discord has to tear families apart
so there can be loving fathers and devoted sons;
it is only in states plagued by troubles
that loyal ministers distinguish themselves. (18)

Abolish wisdom, banish intelligence,
the people will turn the situation to their advantage!
Ban goodness and equity,
the people will be loving and devoted!
Prohibit industry and profit,
not a single crook will be left in the country!
Those three precepts, stated thus, only half
        satisfy me.
I would add these maxims so that they can be
        followed:
"Illustrate candor, embrace simplicity,
limit your ambitions and restrain your desires." (19)

Abandon study to be without cares.*
What is the difference between yes and oh yeah,
Is it so far from the beautiful to the ugly?
Must I not be at all afraid of what frightens others?

---

*Many Chinese scholars, Gao Heng among them, think that this sentence belongs to the preceding section and was moved to section 20 following an erroneous cut when the ancient continuous text was divided into parts in the early Han. The Guodian manuscript seems to confirm this hypothesis.

Nevertheless, vague, confused, it stretches to
    infinity.
They delight and indulge themselves,
revelers feasting at a great sacrifice,
idlers climbing a tower in spring.
I alone am impassive,
like an oracle bone without cracks.
I am the newborn who has not yet laughed.
Light, I wander as though homeless.
Everyone has more than they need,
I alone have lost everything,
because I have retained my innocence.
My mind is confused, confused!
The crowd is enlightened,
only I am in the dark.
I am swept along with the wind and fluctuate
    like the sea.
They know how to do everything, only I am
    impervious.
Why so solitary?
Because I still nurse from my mother. (20)

High Virtue's characteristic
is to proceed from the Way.
In the universe of things, the Way
is evanescent, elusive.
Evanescent and murky,
it harbors within an image.
Evanescent and murky,
it harbors within an object.

Indistinct and dark,
it harbors within an essence.
This essence is very real
because the truth is in it.

From long ago to the present day*
the Name alone never fails,
and thanks to it
the patriarchs may be traced back to the beings.†
How do I know that is so of the patriarchs?
From this. (21)

---

*Like some other existing versions, the text reads "From today until long ago," which slightly changes the meaning of the phrase "The name (*tao*) was assigned in the present but characterizes the Principle's action since the dawn of time"; however, since the expression "From today until long ago" is totally incongruous in translation, I have chosen to keep the traditional formulation.

†In place of *fu*, an honorific designation for when a young man adopts an adult cap, and by extension, "eminent," "debut," the Mawangdui manuscript has the homonym *fu*, meaning "father," and by extension, "ancestor," for which the character *fu*, "eminent," can also be a phonic substitute. The expression *chung-fu* is the standard designation for the lineage of high lords. That is why the *Chuang Tzu* presents a recluse named Hsü-yü who tries to dissuade the sage Yao from ceding his throne to a certain Gap-Tooth, whose disciple he is, by saying to him: "There is the clan ancestor and the lineage ancestor; Gap-Tooth could be a father of the masses [members of the lineage group] (*chung-fu*) but not the father of the fathers of the masses of the members of the lineage group (*chung-fu fu*)." That is to say, he could be the clan ancestor and not the primordial lineage ancestor from whom all the various clan ancestors descend. Chapter 9 of the *Ho Kuan Tzu* also uses the same expression, *chung-fu*, "the fathers of the lineage," as periphrasis for the lords who also happen to be head of the colleges of ancestor worship as eldest sons of the eldest branch of a clan group. Thus by referring to the categories of religion comprised of ancestor worship, the phrase designates the transcendent entities from which diverse phenomena issued.

Who does not fall over standing on tiptoe?
Who can travel farther by lengthening his stride?
Whoever shows off lacks radiance,
whoever struts about does not shine,
whoever boasts does not succeed,
whoever is full of himself does not last.
From the perspective of the Way, all these means
are trash or tumors
that men detest.
The sage who follows the Way stays clear of
    them. (24)

Whatever bends remains unbroken,
whatever curves remains straight,
whatever is hollow refills itself,
whatever wears out renews itself.
Whoever clings gently profits;
whoever clings tightly has a poor grasp.
The sage is content with holding the One,
in order to be the empire's pastor.*
By not showing off, he has radiance,
by not strutting, he shines,
by not boasting, he succeeds,
by not being full of himself, he endures,
rivaling no one, he provokes no rivalry.
Thus we see that the ancient watchword,

---

*Here, the Mawangdui manuscript reads *mu,* "pastor" and by extension,
"head," "leader," in place of *she,* "model," "norm," as in the standard versions.

"Preserve your integrity by bending," is not empty:
by maintaining your integrity you return. (22)

Speaking little is in the order of things:
high winds will not last the morning,
or downpours more than a day.
And even so, who produced them? Heaven and
    Earth.
If the action of the elements does not last,
what does that say about the work of humans?
Whoever serves the Tao becomes one with it,
whoever wins becomes one with profit,*
whoever loses becomes one with loss.
The Tao gives to whomever becomes one with
    profit
and withdraws from whomever becomes one
    with loss. (23)

It was something indistinct,
born before Heaven and Earth.
Dark and murky,
solitary, self-sufficient,
shielded from transformations.†
I regard it as the Mother of the universe.

---

*The standard versions next include a sequence omitted in the two Mawangdui manuscripts: "Whoever becomes one with the Way, the Way welcomes, one with Virtue [or profit?], Virtue welcomes, whoever becomes one with loss, loss welcomes."

†This text omits the following phrase: "It completes an endless course without ever collapsing," as appears in the received text.

Not knowing its name,
I have called it "the Way."
If it was really necessary to give it one,
I would name it "great."
Great, it expands,
expanding, it goes far.
Whatever goes far returns.
The Tao is great,
Heaven is great,
Earth is great,
the king is great.
There are four greats in a country
and the king is one of them.
Man models himself on the Earth,
Earth on Heaven, Heaven on the Tao,
and the Tao on itself. (25)

Heavy, root of the light,
quiet, master of the unstable.
The sage, throughout the journey,
never quits the heavy carriage.
Despite stops at the inns,
he remains peaceful, far from the crowd.*
Can the master of ten thousand carts
be light in the face of the world?
Light, he loses the root;
unstable, he loses the mastery. (26)

---

*This version differs from the standard text, which reads: "Despite grandiose spectacles, he maintains his serenity and stays calm." The Mawangdui text seems better to me, because the travel metaphor is thus extended.

Whoever excels in walking leaves no tracks,
whoever knows how to speak has faultless
    discourse,
whoever knows how to count does not need an
    abacus,
whoever really knows how to retreat is beyond
    locks.
Whoever knows the art of binding, without rope
    or string,
makes knots that no one can untie.
If the sage helps men,
it is because he rejects no one;
if he knows how to soothe beings,
it is because he despises none.
That is what is called being enlightened.
The good man is master of the bad man,
the bad man the material of the good man.
Whoever does not revere his master,
whoever does not care for his material,
however clever, goes astray.
That is the essential secret. (27)

Know the masculine,
guard the feminine,
be the ravine of the world.
Whoever is the ravine of the world
is forever attached to Virtue;
whoever is attached to Virtue

returns to the state of the nursing babe.
Know glory, guard shame,
be the ravine of the world;
whoever is the ravine of the world
will have his fill of Virtue:
whoever has his fill of Virtue
returns to the state of rough wood.
Know white, guard black,
you will be the world's standard;
to the world's standard,
Virtue is never lacking;
Virtue never lacking in him,
he returns to the limitless.
Rough wood, carved, provides tools.
The sage, put to use, is head of the officials.
The supreme Maker never carves anything. (28)

Whoever wants to seize the empire for his own
     gain
is going to meet with failure, I know.
The empire is a sacred vessel that no one can
     wear out.
Whoever uses it breaks it, whoever seizes it loses it.
Beings sometimes lead, sometimes follow,
sometimes they inhale, [sometimes they exhale,
sometimes they flourish, sometimes*] they
     languish,

---

*The text is no doubt faulty; it is corrected here by completing it according
to the standard versions.

sometimes they are erect, sometimes slumped.
The sage is wary of excess, immoderation, luxury. (29)

Whoever assists the sovereign with strategic arts
must not incite him to dominate the princes
    through arms,
because war calls for war.
There are only brambles there where armies
    camp.
His objectives attained, the good general stops.
He conquers nothing by force.
He achieves everything without arrogance.
He achieves everything without ostentation.
He achieves everything without boastfulness.
He achieves everything but prides himself on
    nothing.
Even if he wins the victory,
he does not try to dominate,
because he knows that peak strength is followed
    by old age,
and that this would be to go against the order of
    things.
Whoever goes against the order of things comes
    to an early end. (30)

Weapons are deadly objects
that all beings hate,
the man of the Way stays clear of them.
Ordinarily the left takes precedence,
with the army it reverts to the right.

Weapons are deadly objects,
they are not part of a sage's arsenal,
he resorts to them only in defending his body.
Prizing serenity above all else,
he does not glory in his high deeds.
To glory in one's high deed is to rejoice in
    killing.
Whoever rejoices in killing will not win the
    votes of the empire.
The left has the place of honor at joyous
    occasions,
the right has the place of honor at funeral
    rites.
The lieutenant general stands on the left,
the highest general stands on the right,
attesting that war is a funeral.
One must weep for the multitudes that one has
    massacred:
any victory is celebrated with funeral rites. (31)

The Way has no name because it is rough
    wood.
As small as it is, no one can enslave it.
If kings and dukes knew how to preserve it,
the whole universe would come to pay them
    homage,
Heaven and Earth would unite their breaths,
a gentle dew would spread over Earth;
with no one commanding them, men
would live in equality and accord.

As soon as there is institution,* there are names.
Once the names are distributed, they assign
    boundaries;†
knowledge of boundaries is a protection from
    danger.
The Way is to beings of the universe
what the seas are to the rivers. (32)

---

*The Chinese word *chih,* translated here as "institution," has the double meaning of "to create," "to manufacture," "to institute," and "to establish a legislative system." The text plays on this double meaning. Just as any legislative system creates a hierarchy of ranks and functions establishing divisions within a social body, any manufacturing process, by cutting, creates distinct objects beginning from the undivided, unformed mass of the raw material. Similarly, the word *ming* designates the words in the language that make arbitrary distinctions in the undifferentiated fabric of phenomenal reality, as well as the titles of offices, social qualifications marking the social division of labor, titles that call for sanctions (possibly legal) as a function of the work accomplished and results achieved. This idea is developed especially in *The Four Canons,* in keeping with the legalist texts.

†Most translators understand *chih* as meaning "to stop," but it also has the meaning of "boundary." The *ming,* the "names" in the double role of "designation of things" and "titles of offices," assign arbitrary boundaries to a continuous, fluid reality, which is at once a loss—loss of spontaneity—and a safeguard, because denominations, as social qualifications, provide a reference point in the universe of constituted forms. The *Chuang Tzu* is interested in this classifying—and arbitrary—aspect of language, particularly in the second chapter, "Discourse on the Identity of Things," which states: "Even though reality itself has no boundaries and speech is not constant, there are those that create boundary markers and boundaries. What are they, please tell me? There are the right and the left, there are categories and judgments, there are divisions and distinctions, there are antagonisms and disputes—such are the eight powers of thought." Wang Pi, moreover, uses the word *chih* in his annotations for the *Lao Tzu,* in the sense of "boundary markers," "boundaries." Thus, in his commentary on section 38, he offers this statement: "Thus, with names are created the divided (*fen*), with objects are established the delimited (*chih*)."

Whoever knows the other is informed,
whoever knows himself is shrewd,
whoever triumphs over others is strong,
whoever triumphs over himself is powerful,
whoever knows how to be content is rich,
whoever makes himself act possesses will.
Whoever remains in his place will endure;
whoever dies without being forgotten is
    immortal. (33)

The Way is like impetuous water,
going to the right, going to the left.*
It works and accomplishes but does not take
    pride in itself;
obtaining allegiance without seeking to
    dominate,
because it has no desires, it can be called
    "minuscule."
Obtaining allegiance without seeking to dominate,
it can also be called "great."
The sage is great for doing nothing to be great
and thus attains grandeur. (34)

Whoever possesses the supreme image
will attract the empire to himself.

---

*The sentence "It provides for the existence of all beings and rejects none of them," which follows in standard editions, is omitted, as is the sentence "It clothes beings without being their master" following "It works and accomplishes but does not take pride in itself."

It will come to him and will be protected from
    misfortune.
Great will be its peace and its joy.
Music and feasting draw the passerby,
but as soon as one speaks of the Way,
everyone cries, "That's dull! That's insipid!"*
Looking at it, it is invisible,
listening to it, it is inaudible,
putting it to use, it is thus inexhaustible. (35)

Increase what you want to reduce,
strengthen what you want to weaken,
raise what you want to demote,
give to the one you would take from,
and you will shine without shadow.
The supple defeats the rigid,
weak defeats strong.
Fish must not leave
the ocean depths;
the weapons of power
must never let themselves be seen. (36)

The Way suffers no designation.†
If only kings and dukes knew how to practice it,
men would educate themselves.

---

*The Mawangdui version adds a *yüeh,* "one says," which makes the sentence
that follows an exclamation of the common people.
†The received text reads: "The way never does anything and there is nothing that it does not do." Here the text seems closer to section 32: "The Way
has no name because it is rough wood."

If, despite education, they were distracted by
    desires,
the simplicity of the Unsayable would know how
    to contain them.
In the simplicity of the Unsayable, desires are
    abolished.
Desires abolished, serenity would reign
and the whole universe would spontaneously rule
    itself. (37)

THE FOUR CANONS
OF THE
YELLOW EMPEROR

CANON I

ON THE LAW AS PRINCIPLE

The Law Way

The Way engenders the Law. The Law traces the dividing line between the true and the false like the string separates the straight from the curved. Let a prince possess the Way and no one will dare to violate the law or let his edicts go unheeded. Provided that he himself draws the string taut, he will see and know the whole empire without ever committing an error.*

---

*The text is a copy of the chapters "The Art of the Mind" and "Taking Law as Model" from the *Kuan Tzu,* a compendium of various texts, for the most part legalist and strategist in nature, dating from the fourth to third centuries BCE. It could thus be understood, as it is by most commentators and translators, as taking up the argument of a passage in the *Kuan Tzu* expressing a related idea: "The prince who conforms to the Tao does not break the law of which he is himself the author; he does not overstep the limits that he has established. Applying the string to himself, he sees and knows the whole empire without ever letting himself abuse it." But I think it is a question here of applying the law generally and not simply the limited problem of the sovereign's respect for the law.

Empty, without form, its appearance is dark, yet from this darkness proceeds the life of all beings.* Whatever undermines life is called "desire," "insatiability." Life leads to movement; any flaw in that movement is called "inopportuneness," or if it takes place at the required time, "incongruity." All movement assumes an activity, any flaw in that activity is called "aberration," "impropriety"; all activity is accompanied by speech, the flaws that mar speech are called "unlikelihood," "impertinence," "boastfulness," "nonsense," or "trying to make incompetence pass for competence."

Even though they issue from the same dark origin, some things live, others die, some succeed, others fail; happiness and misfortune follow the same paths, no one knows where they come from.

The only means of knowing: to be empty, without determination. Because within the void of not-having, as soon as one atom is made, there are forms and names. Once forms and names are established, white and black are distinguished. Thus the one who possesses the Way examines the world by being without opinion, unconfined to place, inactive, without partiality.

Whatever matters arise, they all take on form and name, designation and appellation. Once forms and names, designations and appellations are established, there is nowhere to hide one's tracks, no way to escape the rules.

Public good is luminous, extreme clarity effective, absolute rectitude serene. Whoever is infinitely serene is a sage;

---

*This describes the Tao. For descriptions of the Tao as the dark and indeterminate origin of the manifested world, see the *Lao Tzu,* sections 1, 14, 21, 25, and 42.

whoever considers the public good is infinitely wise; whoever is infinitely wise is the touchstone of the universe.*

One uses a scale for weighing, finds one's bearings with a compass; when some matter arises, everything is regulated for the best. Matters arise dense as trees in a forest, numerous as grain in the granaries; as soon as the measures of length and capacity are established, nothing escapes their divine authority. That is why it is said: "Measures and standards in place, one can govern and suppress his subjects."

It renews what is undone, restores what is destroyed, where does its omnipotence end? It returns a dead body to life, it transforms misfortune into happiness, who knows its limits? Is it not in returning to the without-form to find it there again that one will discover the origin of happiness and misfortune?

The Way that allows for responding to any circumstance resides in the scales. As soon as one stops calibrating weight, one loses the Way. Heaven and Earth have unchanging laws, the people have permanent occupations: nobles and commoners have immutable positions. There is a single way to pay subjects their salaries and a fixed measure for employing them. The invariable laws of Heaven and Earth: the changing of the seasons, dark and light, life and death, solid and liquid; the permanent occupations of the people: plowing for men, weaving for women; the immutable positions of commoners and nobles: men of much and men of little do not encroach upon

---

*This entire passage is very close to the fifth chapter of the *Han Fei Tzu,* "The Way of the Master": "Empty, inactive, it waits: the names are named, the classes are given. Empty, it penetrates the reality of emotions, inactive, it is the regulator of action," and so on.

one another; the single way to pay subjects: give work to competent men, watching that they do not exceed their abilities; the fixed measure for employing them: forgo personal interests for the sake of the general good.

Changing the constant laws, altering the standards, will make it necessary to resort to exceptional measures to rule. Regular and irregular processes must each play their part so that the names do not escape. In small as in great matters, each individual finds his place; docile or rebellious, provider of life or provider of death, each being is spontaneously designated. Forms and names established, the beings regulate themselves.

The sage who has apprehended the Tao, enlightened by the cyclical movement of Heaven, understands the relationships between prince and subjects. He deeply grasps the origin and the end of all things and nevertheless does not try to dominate. Exceedingly pure, immaculate and impalpable, he is the regulator of the universe.

The Good Order of a Country

If the good order is flouted, the nation is shaken to its core. If the prince takes without giving, the country is immediately headed for collapse. Whoever does not know how to take full advantage of reversals risks seeing the rival principality reborn from its ashes, having not been destroyed. The one who inflicts punishment upon a prince who does not deserve it exposes himself to misfortune! But whoever launches an expedition to punish a guilty prince destined for ruin and then, after reducing his capital to ashes, annexes his states without claiming his territory, he makes himself the executor of providence.

Heaven and Earth are impartial, the four seasons follow one another without pause. In their image, the sage supports and shelters all beings. But the one who goes counter to the celestial movement and does not respect its measure exposes himself to its wrath. When the opposing power is strong enough to prevail over circumstances, try to avoid it and be careful not to stand up to it! But as soon as circumstances prevail over it, one must know how to act in concert with them. One retreats to better deploy; one is careful to take full advantage of the opportunity without taking credit for what belongs to the immutable course of things.

The one who, having annexed the states of another prince, reinforces his walls, occupies his palaces, lets himself be charmed by the tones of his orchestras, enjoys his riches, and possesses his wives puts the country in peril and exposes himself to ruin through this dissolute behavior contrary to reason. That is why only the sage knows how to take advantage of reversals in fortune and to make use of favorable circumstances. Heaven and Earth authorize no more than three consecutive successes. Whoever has achieved exploits does not know how to stop short of misfortune.

When the sage conducts a punitive expedition, once the guilty prince's country is annexed, he razes its walls, destroys its instruments, distributes its riches, sends away the wives, dissolves the states, offering them exclusively to deserving subjects. That is what is called doing heavenly work. Whoever accomplishes these deeds without fail need not fear the blows of fate.

Do not upstage yang, do not upstage yin, do not exhaust your subjects in the earthworks, do not exasperate men, do not promote factions. Heaven conceals its brightness from the one who upstages yang, Earth becomes barren when one upstages yin, whoever exhausts his subjects in the earthworks summons war, whoever exasperates men prompts their exodus, wherever factions confront one another, the external and internal collide.

Exacerbating yang causes epidemics, exacerbating yin causes famine; exhausting men in the earthworks leads to the loss of territories, vexing people leads to their flight, factional conflicts are the source of troubles. These are called the Five Aberrations. Whoever accrues the Five Aberrations concurrently [puts his country in peril; the sovereign who wants to undermine*] natural rules, change customs, wildly alter practices, exert discretionary power, and change laws according to his pleasure, the prince who would thus indulge his desire to conduct himself in this way exposes himself to the worst misfortunes. This is called overreaching celestial heights and losing the measure.

The Regulatory Power of the Sovereign

The first year one follows the customs, the second he extends his generosity, the third the people experience ease, the fourth he pronounces edicts, the fifth he applies corrective punishments, the sixth he elicits fear, the seventh he is in a position to lead a campaign. By letting the people follow the customs the first year, he studies his means; by distributing wealth the second year, he stimulates zeal; because there is relief from drudgery and taxes the third year, the people make gains; the

---

*The text is corrupt; it is completed here according to the probable meaning.

fourth year he elicits fear by pronouncing laws; the fifth year he applies corrective punishments, so that the people know they must not rely on luck; the sixth year, [since he knows how to inspire fear, the people fully obey]; the seventh year he is in a position to lead a campaign because he is sure of overcoming the adversary, no matter how powerful.

The customs follow the people's inclinations, generosity stimulates them, gains are obtained through lifting prohibitions and lowering customs duties; instituting laws means organizing the population into brigades* and selecting those with talent, allowing the capable to be distinguished from the incapable; making use of punishments to correct the people consists of applying capital punishment unremittingly [. . .]. And if, after taking these measures, one can lead a punitive campaign, it is because, thanks to them, the people are ready to sacrifice their lives.

Provided that one issues edicts, the people will be united among themselves and with their leaders; they will share the same conduct and the same heart; if nothing turns subordinates against their superiors, the people will have no second thoughts, and they can be used in defense of the cities as well as in pitched battles.

It is thanks to customs that newly issued edicts are flawlessly executed; it is through love for their prince that men

---

*Beginning in the second half of the fourth century, in all principalities in China, the population was divided into territorial hierarchies beginning from the basic unit of the five-man brigade, collectively responsible and subject to mutual espionage. The whole passage is inspired by the legalists who developed the theory of absolutist power and attacked the foundations of the centralized institutions, which ensured the stability of imperial rule.

and women are inspired to work; it is because he knows the opportune moment that the people obey when their master commands them to act or to rest; it is because he distributes rewards and punishments advisedly that subjects accept them with neither gratitude nor acrimony.

In distinguishing the noble from the commoner, one marks the distance separating the man of much from the man of little. And by assigning to each condition its distinctive signs, the noble and the base are hierachized. If there are neither crooks nor thieves in a country, if lying and treachery are unknown, if the people do not harbor corrupt thoughts, it is because they have enough of everything and punishments are dealt advisedly. No defense conducted with surplus force can be weakened; any attack led with insufficient means will backfire on the assailant.

As beautiful and dead seasons follow one another in the firmament, the prince alternates rewards and punishments in his government. When, in the image of Heaven, which dispenses life, the sovereign protects and nourishes, the State fulfills its civil functions; when following the example of Heaven, which makes things perish, he punishes and inflicts death, the State exercises its military prerogatives. Provided that a prince knows how to use civil and military procedures jointly, he will make the universe obey him.

Man's foundation is found in the Earth, Earth's foundation is found in the correctness of the soils, the correctness of the soils is dependent on the cycle of the seasons, the correct use of the seasons depends upon the people, the efficacy of the people resides in their zeal for work, their zeal for work lies in its regulation.

Whoever knows the nature of the soils knows how to plant at the required time, makes use of the people by conserving their strength, and will contribute to the increase of goods; moreover, if the taxes and duties are reasonable, the people will experience ease; living in abundance, they will have a sense of shame; having a sense of shame, the laws and edicts will become custom, so that there will be no need to resort to punishments. As soon as the law becomes custom, rendering sanctions useless, the country is solid in defense and victorious in offense.

A State has no better regulatory tools than laws and norms; a country governed by means of laws and norms will not fall prey to disorder, provided that the authors of the laws themselves find it impossible to disturb them. The order of the State is ensured when rewards and punishments are distributed judiciously by impartial magistrates who have only the public good in mind. Civil peace is established by alleviating drudgery, reducing taxes, letting the people attend to their work.

A father who does not act as a father cannot hope for his son to serve him as a son; without the goodness of a mother, the sovereign cannot make the people devote the best of their strength to him. It is only when one simultaneously possesses the virtues of a father and a mother that he can dispense the blessings of Heaven and Earth.

It is only when the three prerequisites are united that one can manage his affairs well. Moreover, when one manages to align himself with the empire's valiant and brave, he will be perfectly guarded. The whole universe swears allegiance to the one who fully fathoms the art of using civil and military means. The people obey orders when they are in accord with their tendencies; they cherish their superiors when their superiors demonstrate a nonexclusive love for all.

The Six Alternatives
Aberrations vs. Normalities

Whoever wants to observe a country observes the prince, whoever wants to observe a family observes the father. Because whoever knows how to govern a country behaves as a prince, whoever knows how to direct a family behaves as a father. When observing a country, it is necessary to be attentive to the "Six Aberrations."*

> When sons usurp the father's role, when ministers usurp the sovereign's role, even the most powerful principality cannot govern.
> When the prince's advisors hold outside positions,† the realm's security is threatened, and if the prince does not

---

*Here the word *ni* is contrasted with its antonym *shun*; they are difficult terms to translate: *ni* simultaneously designates unnatural behavior, aberrant phenomena or acts, and a rebellious attitude, while *shun* connotes all that is normal and part of the natural course of things; it can also mean "docile." Sometimes they could almost be rendered as "good" and "bad," or even "normal" and "pathological." These two ideas play a fundamental role in *The Four Canons of the Yellow Emperor* and form two large classificatory rubrics for natural phenomena and human behavior.

†Often during the Warring States Period, ministers received appointments from other princes and they sometimes happened to be in the service of many powers at the same time. Thus Su Ch'in, one of the most visible statesmen in the late fourth century, was a minister for six states at one time!

perceive this, his altars to the gods of the soil and the harvests risk being destroyed.

As soon as the sovereign no longer fulfills his function, the country finds itself spineless, but provided that the ministers perform their tasks, the subordinates will have a base upon which they can depend, so that the nation will go through difficulties but will survive.

When the sovereign does not fulfill his function, the country goes adrift.

If the ministers do not perform their tasks, orders are no longer carried out; then the State is in decay.

When a country has two masters, its policies will not be clear; where the woman struggles with the man for preeminence, the army is disorganized. Such principalities are headed for ruin.

When the crown prince replaces his father, dissension rules at the head of the State; the throng of dignitaries renounces the reigning house. When a minister takes control of the State, the sovereign finds himself isolated. In such a case, a great principality will be diminished, an average one will be subjected to serious setbacks, a small one will be destroyed.

When the prince's advisors hold outside positions, thus hindering affairs from running smoothly, the principality risks unrest; in such a case, a great principality will experience difficulties, an average one will be diminished, a small one will be subject to painful setbacks.

When the sovereign neglects his duties, but the dignitaries

fulfill their offices, the State remains propped up despite everything, as long as the country is content to border on misfortune. In such a case, a great principality will have worries, an average one will experience difficulties, a small one will be diminished.

When neither the sovereign fulfills his function nor the ministers perform their tasks, so that there is no longer a trunk, and so that from top to bottom, all of society finds itself deprived of a solid base, the country risks being seriously weakened. In such a case, a great principality will suffer a painful setback, an average one will be on the way to ruin, a small one will be annihilated.

When the sovereign is cruel and his ministers careless, the country will go to the dogs. There are armies within as well as without and Heaven will surely inflict great misfortunes. No matter how powerful the country where such a situation prevails, it is destined for certain ruin.

When a country has two masters, that is, when the man and the woman dispute over authority, the government is led astray and armies camp within the capital itself. In such a case, the great principality suffers a painful setback, an average power is destined to disappear, a small one is annihilated.

In the same way, when one observes a country, one must be attentive to the "Six Normalities."

As long as a sovereign maintains his rank, the country has a solid base at its disposal.

Even if the ministers neglect their offices, depriving the

subordinates of all firm ties, the nation's suffering will not threaten its existence.

A country with a magnanimous sovereign and loyal ministers knows peace.

A country where the prince acts as prince, the ministers as ministers, and good intelligence reigns between subordinates and superiors is strong.

A country where the sovereign respects the law and where the ministers comply with the norm flourishes.

A country where the sovereign holds his rank and obtains the support of the ministers will rule over the world.

The Six Aberrations and the Six Normalities draw the dividing line between survival and extinction, between grandeur and decadence. Provided that the sovereign chooses options that satisfy these Six Alternatives, he will put the power of life and death to use judiciously, rewarding deserving subjects and dealing the guilty ones decisive blows. As a result, peace will reign. He will correct his subjects through his brilliant virtue; and, forming a triad with Heaven and Earth, perfectly impartial, he will support and protect all beings, embracing them in the same universal love. That is how he will be able to rule over the empire. The method for governing the world: to win the support of Heaven, Earth, and men. Yes, whoever knows how to use these three authorities is the absolute master of the universe.

When the sovereign sits enthroned facing south, inspiring such respect from his ministers that they are careful to stay in his shadow, when their subordinates in turn are docile and obedient, not daring to conceal anything from their superiors, when the people, happy to serve their masters, live in harmony, then he is assured of having at his disposal vast territories, large populations, and powerful armies, so that he is unrivaled throughout the empire. Dispensing the benefits of civil government even to the most humble, applying military rigor to the most powerful: this, in essence, constitutes the king's craft. Without knowing the secrets of it, one will not be able to reign.

The prince instructed in the art of governing devotes himself to the hunt without forgetting his duties, tastes the joy of banquets without succumbing to drunkenness, diverts himself with his wives and trinkets without being led astray. At war with the lords, he wins victories at little cost, [and victorious, his orders are obeyed*]; [at peace with his neighbors†], the country is rich and the people [numerous]; [sages sojourn in such a realm and the princes are its allies‡].

But on the other hand, the one who does not know this art devotes himself wildly to hunting, gets drunk during banquets, is led astray by his wives and trinkets, wins few victories at great cost when he goes to war with the lords and, even when he is victorious, his orders [are not obeyed . . .]. If he is at peace with his neighbors, then the country is poor and the people neglect their occupations. Sages do not sojourn in such a realm; the feudal princes are not its allies. If moreover the sovereign has no consideration for the literati and is not

---

*Completed according to the parallel opposing sentence regarding the sovereign who does not possess the art of governing.
†Completed according to principle of parallelism, following the suggestion of the Chinese scholar Chen Guying.
‡Completed again according to the same principle.

schooled by those who know the art of government, there is little doubt that his realm will fall to another.

But if the prince possesses mysterious Virtue,* if he possesses [. . .] and if he alone knows [. . .], he will govern the empire without anyone understanding the methods of his action. The sovereign willing to sacrifice his provinces to honor the valiant will have a powerful country at his disposal and will know security; whoever cares less about his goods than wise advisors will be rich and honored; whoever knows

---

*This expression appears in section 65 of the *Tao Te Ching,* which defines it in the following way: "Those who used to possess the Way did not use it to enlighten the people but to make them dimmer. What makes people rebellious is excessive cleverness. Whoever governs a country through reason commits a crime against it; whoever governs it without bright ideas is its benefactor. Keeping this opposition ever in mind is the standard and the compass on which to model oneself. Always knowing the standard and the compass is to possess mysterious Virtue." In chapter 10, "The Supreme Confusion," of the *Ho Kuan Tzu,* a text dating from the late third century BCE, the same expression is used in relationship to the law, in a sequence very similar to those in sections of *The Four Canons.* Thus, let us provide a long extract: "The law is the regulatory instrument of Heaven and Earth. If one does not use the law advisedly, he cannot perfect mysterious Virtue. The wisest sage is in harmony with Heaven and Earth, he ties the six knots so solidly that nothing can undo them. Facing south, he firmly embraces the Principle, surrounded by transcendent entities that flank him on the right and on the left, in front and behind, while, as a fountain of justice that spills into an impetuous wave, he presides at the center, impassive. His regulatory influence, invisible and subtle, spreads throughout the world in an endless, majestic give-and-take, applying the string to all. He maintains the web for those within; those without, he ensnares in the net of the law. He always acts in conformity with the logic of things and the opportunity of the moment. He regulates the beings that succeed one another in an orderly cycle, each having a beginning and an end. He unifies and centralizes the various tasks and establishes clear-sighted committees, the five matrixes and the four seasons each following its order and its class."

how to humble himself to receive the sages will find himself revered and his orders obeyed. [The sovereign who knows how to treat the literati] of the empire will be a model for the empire.

That prince is a hegemon who keeps the valiant at his court and makes the rebels repent, inflicts just punishment upon the troublemakers without trying to seize their wealth; that is how he commands the empire without anyone daring to disobey him. Below the hegemons, all those who fight with weapons and seek to dominate through force are destined for quick ruin, although none can comprehend how misfortune has befallen them.

To characterize in a word the exercise of sovereign power, [...] I would say that only the true king knows how to support and protect all the subjects in the empire so that all things arrive at their perfect completion.

The Four Rules
Being Calm, Regulated, Civil, and Martial

When the sovereign and the minister exchange places, there is disorder, when the sages and the fools occupy analogous positions, there is confusion, when activity and rest are out of rhythm, there is aberration, when the power of life and death is applied randomly, there is savagery.

Disorder shakes the foundations, confusion disturbs matters, aberration thwarts Heaven, savagery alienates men; when the foundations are shaken, the country is diminished, when tasks are neglected, the country is invaded, when Heaven is thwarted, there is famine, when men are alienated, there is rancor. Heaven provides the standard of cyclical movement. This mode of action is not in the least remote; it commands our waking and our sleeping.

> The country is calm when prince and subjects are in their places;
> it is regulated when capable and incapable are ranked according to their merit;
> it is civil when the sovereign models the times of activity and rest on the cycle of Heaven and Earth;
> martial when he strikes advisedly and at the opportune time.
> Impassive, he brings peace;
> regulated, he makes order reign;
> civil, he is clear-sighted;
> martial, he is powerful.

Peace guarantees the stability of the foundations, order the harmony of men, clear-sightedness the aid of Heaven, power prestige. As soon as the prince forms a triad with Heaven and Earth, as soon as he is in harmony with his subjects and combines civil and military measures, he achieves the Great Union. The prince who has deeply absorbed the Four Rules will be able to pacify the empire and bring peace to his realm.

The success of one who applies adequate measures within but imposes inopportune policies without will cause him harm; the success of one who applies inopportune measures within but imposes adequate policies without will lead to his death. The one who imposes aberrant policies within as without will have a double share of misfortune; he will be executed and his principality destroyed. Whoever imposes policies conforming within and without to Heaven is in harmony; if, successes achieved, he does not flag in his efforts, his descendants will be favored by fate. That glory and renown [respond to reality is the mark] of efficacy; all action must be in accord; rectitude is the root of matters.

Respect the course of the world and adhere to the order of things by starting from the beginning. Make conformity the maxim of your action, punish whoever deserves punishment, and you will always be in harmony with reason. Whoever breaks his contracts will be hounded; whoever abolishes punishments exposes himself to torment; avoid going in the opposite direction to be ever in harmony: should some failing occur, even if you do not achieve success, Heaven will spare you the blows of fate.

[Do not abuse your power of death by taking innocent lives]; do not abuse your power of life by sparing death; do not cloak yourself in vainglory, because the renown of one who enjoys a usurped reputation is destined to disappear. Inflict death at the height of yang, dispense life at the height of yin, that is called acting against the decrees of yin and yang; dispense death outside the height of yang, dispense life within the height of yin, that not only opposes the cycle of yin and yang but also reverses their respective positions. Whoever acts in such a way calls down misfortune upon himself, if he does not bring about his realm's downfall. [Because it is fitting to dispense death in accord with yin and ensure life in accord with yang.*]

---

*The eight missing characters completed here according to the conjectures of Leo S. Chang and Yu Feng.

[Standards] exist so that one measure is appropriate. Everything arriving at its height begins its return, declines having reached its peak. That is how the universe functions, the great law at work among men; whether normal or aberrant, all acts participate in the same course of things, even if they obey opposing principles. Knowing how to recognize the normal and the aberrant, that is called possessing the standard of the Tao.

What country will not be subjugated by one who is strong and knows how to bow before the weak? Who will not be won over by one who occupies a high position and knows how to bow to the humble? What [success will not be achieved] when the man of much knows how to yield to the man of little?

The compass provides the circle, the square the square, the string the straight line, the plumb line the perpendicular, the level the horizontal, the foot the length, the scale the weight, the bushel the quantity; these eight measures are the standards of daily life; the movements of the stars, the sun and the moon as well as the constellations, the cycle of the seasons, the times of activity and rest, the distinction between within and without, all that provides the heavenly standard.

Thanks to the earthly standard, high and the low remain visible, fertile and barren lands contrast; thanks to the human standards, prince and subjects hold their ranks, the literati attend to their occupations, each is given employment not exceeding his abilities, the common good takes precedence over special interests. As soon as good and evil have adequate qualifiers, as soon as normal and aberrant behaviors are manifest, as soon as truth and lie take on reality, the sovereign possesses the standard and through this means becomes the regulator of the universe.

Military measures consist of punishing those Heaven has destined for ruin by acting at the opportune time. In order to be crowned with success, these measures must be accompanied by civil means. Only the prince who has twice as many civil as military means will rule over the empire. The prince who persists in using means to rule that offend reason and lives in madness and mental distraction without mending his ways exposes himself to the most terrible punishments. Faintheartedness consists of dreading the future when one has not the least fault worthy of reproach and of trembling even before misfortune strikes. That is true weakness. Whoever is stiff and straight [. . .].

When one's renown corresponds to deeds accomplished, he will enjoy long life; but when renown does not correspond to merit, when the words override reality, then one has lost the Way and risks suffering a grievous death. The heaps of gold and jade that the prince accumulates in his coffers bring resentment; the bands of musicians with which he surrounds himself, the pleasures in which he loses himself are the harbingers of disorder. How can you hope that advisors, as wise as they are, can draw up plans for you when you protect the bringers of resentment and look after the harbingers of disorder?

Evaluations

The master of men is the [replica] of Heaven and Earth, the source of laws and edicts, the fate [of the people]; if he did not make Heaven his Heaven, he would lose his power; if he did not lend his weight to Earth, he would lose his roots; if he did not follow the cycle of the seasons, the people would suffer from it;* if he did not define internal and external, if he did not respond to the phases of activity and rest, business would be botched within and undertakings would fail without [. . .]; if the Eight Regulators† are neglected [. . .]; but if he takes Heaven for Heaven, divine efficiency is at his disposal, if he lends his weight to the Earth, he has solid roots, if he follows the cycles of the seasons, [. . .] and the people no longer have to [. . .] or to suffer. If he defines internal and external,‡ if he responds to the phases of activity and rest, business is conducted well within and enterprises succeed without.

When the Eight Regulators suffer no deficiencies, the sovereign will endure as long as Heaven and Earth. Holding the One, Heaven makes the Three Lights shine,§ determines the Two Principles,¶ establishes the Eight Regulators, applies the Seven Laws, so that [. . .] amid [and nothing can . . .]. Everything that walks, crawls, flies, breathes, moves, thanks to the unicity of Heaven [. . .] and perseveres in its being.

That is how Heaven, holding the One, makes the Three Lights shine. The sun appears and disappears at fixed times following a programmed orbit and indicates the farthest positions of the North and South poles through the solstices,

---

*Or else "would curse him," the word *chi* having the two meanings of "to suffer," and "to detest."

†The Eight Regulators are the four seasons (spring, summer, winter, fall), activity and rest, and within and without.

‡This refers to the two spheres of the inner palace, that is, the sovereign's immediate circle, and the civil administration as well as the military system.

§That is, the sun, the moon, and the stars.

¶That is, yin and yang. As for the Seven Laws, a bit further on the text explains what is meant by them, though only six are given, the text being defective.

providing the standard for measurements. The moon wanes to be invariably reborn, according to unchanging phases of growth and decline, offering the model for computing time. Without deviating from their course, without running into one another, the stars move in orderly fashion, providing the standard of regularity.*

Heaven makes the Three Lights shine in order to determine the Two Principles, that is how light alternates with dark [. . .]. It determines the Two Principles in order to establish the Eight Regulators, so that the four seasons have their order, activity and rest their time, within and without their place.

Once the Eight Regulators are established, the Seven Laws are put to work. That is how Heaven is luminous and regular in its action, congruent in its standard, exact in its phases, cyclical in its nature, inescapable in its decrees [. . .], that is how it commands all beings in creation. Such are the Seven Laws.

When the Seven Laws correspond to their description, there is enterprise.† We call "principle of order" the fact that each enterprise [. . .]. We call "conformity" the presence of the principle of order in an enterprise. We say that an enterprise has lost the principle of order when it no longer conforms to the course of things. We call "aberration" any departure from the norm. Once both the states of conformity and aberration have been clearly defined, it becomes possible to predict with certainty: growth and decline, survival and extinction.

---

*An identical passage appears in the *Ho Kuan Tzu,* in chapter 9, "On Sovereign Power."

†The Chinese word translated here as "enterprise" is *wu,* usually rendered as "being" or "thing," but which also means "business," "undertaking," or even "function"; this seems to be the meaning that must be understood here.

Power engenders authority, authority indulgence, indulgence rectitude, rectitude calm, calm peace, peace stability, stability candor, candor acuity, acuity penetration; once the height of penetration is achieved, understanding can no longer go astray.

The first kings and emperors knew how to master this art. Possessing the secret of universal mechanics, having Heaven's own acuity, they scanned the spaces extending to the four ends of the Earth; grasping the Six Levers, they commanded the whole world; possessing a deep knowledge of the Three Denominations, they could rule over the ten thousand beings; thanks to their intimate familiarity with the principles that preside over the normal and the aberrant, they understood the causes that explain the rise and fall of empires, going back to the source upon which full and empty, movement and rest depend; and as they understood the obvious fact that the denominations must respond to reality, they could distinguish between true and false without ever committing mistakes. That is how they did royal work.

The Six Levers are as follows: the first is named "examination," the second "evaluation," the third "action," the fourth "reversal,"* the fifth "deployment,"† the sixth "transformation."‡

---

*The Chinese term is *ch'uan,* which means "to achieve a complete turn." It must undoubtedly be seen in relationship here with the term *fan,* "reversal," used by the *Han Fei Tzu,* which denotes investigative techniques that reveal the truth alleging the false.

†The word *pien* is hard to interpret. It means "mutation," "transformation," "change," but in texts on strategy it also has the meaning of either "deployment" of troop formations or "trap."

‡The term *hua,* "transformative action," denotes the civilizing influence of the sovereign on the people.

Examination lets us detect the countries destined to endure or to disappear, evaluation lets us know the causes of greatness and decline, action lets us destroy the powerful and aid the weak, reversal lets us make [the division] between true and false, deployment lets us punish the one who should perish and support the one who deserves to live, transformation lets us make virtue shine forth and eradicate vice. The one who fully possesses the Six Levers can be assured of reigning over the world.

The Three Denominations are as follows: the first is called "correct denominations," they ensure the order of the hierarchy; the second "incorrect denominations," they result in disorders in legislation; the third "nonexistent denominations," they inevitably lead to the sovereign's fall, all powerful as he is. As soon as the Three Denominations are clear, all enterprises can be conducted in a satisfactory manner.

Reversing the times of activity and rest, growing regardless of the soil conditions, is to violate the order of Heaven and Earth. When his subjects do not cherish their prince, when subordinates have no affection for their superiors, when guild members neglect their tasks, the people violate the internal order. Such a country is destined for ruin; it deserves to be punished. The one that adopts the opposite path conforms with the order; it is destined to endure; a country destined to endure deserves to be supported. The two kinds of nations that practice correct or aberrant policies call for different treatments; that is why it is good to have perfect mastery of true and false.

Pretend to be empty when you are full; make believe that you have everything when you have nothing. If some trouble arises with your neighbor, raise an army against him and the empire will bite your hand; if the world is without trouble, cultivate peace at home and the empire will remain quiet. If the names do not respond to reality, remain calm. If the names do not respond to reality, be at peace.* Things offer themselves, names name themselves, affairs order themselves;† once the Three Denominations are clarified, one untangles the true from the false without being taken in. A country governed according to these principles will flourish; the principality that exposes itself to that country's just wrath will immediately perish.

Factors of Ruin

Any violation of prohibitions, any offense against the standard is inevitably sanctioned by Heaven. A country accrues the Six Dangers and it is annihilated, the Three Injustices and it perishes, it ignores edicts and it is destined to disappear. If the sovereign of a State is victim of the Three Confinements, then he will see his territories annexed and will be overturned; if he gives himself over to the Three Evils, he will draw misfortune down upon himself.‡

---

*There is clearly a transcription error in these two phrases, as the meaning is not very satisfactory.

†Compare this with chapter 5 of the *Han Fei Tzu*, "The Way of the Master": "Empty, inactive, he waits: the names name themselves, the classes order themselves. Empty, he penetrates the reality of emotions. Inactive, he is the regulator of action. Whoever speaks, names; whoever acts manifests the Form. Names and Forms matched, classed, the prince has no business to attend to: he returns to the depths of being."

‡[The Dangers, Injustices, Confinements, and Evils mentioned here are elaborated in the following text. —*Ed.*]

Arrogance leads to the death of kings and the punishment of subjects. The one whose exploits exceed his virtues will experience downfall; he will perish, the one who, stripped of the power to attribute to things their names, is incapable of being king.* Whoever covets riches, does not respect his engagements, does not apply punishments, is a troublemaker, or attracts resentment, who thus renders himself guilty of one of those five faults exposes himself to misfortune.

The country that counts upon fortified passes for its defense will be diminished, the one that banks on military power alone will be weakened; Heaven will heap double shares of misfortune on whoever raises armies without reason and punishes the innocent. However, until contrary signs appear, the guilty one still enjoys Heaven's indulgence, but as soon as contrary signs appear, Heaven will not prolong his life for an instant and will punish him with doubled severity.†

A great sovereign retains his serenity when he rises to the

---

*The meaning of this phrase in Chinese is very ambiguous. It could be "the sovereign whose reputation is overshadowed," as Robin D. S. Yates understands it, or "the sovereign who has lost the prerogative of conferring official titles," as Leo S. Chang and Yu Fen translate it. But it seems to me a matter of the more general power of giving names to things. The *Chuang Tzu* and the *Ho Kuan Tzu* use the periphrasis *ming-shih,* "the master of names," to designate the monarch. Sovereign power is manifested essentially in the power to give things their names. Thus the eunuch Chao Kao, prime minister for the second emperor, knew that he was the true master when he could call a stag a horse and no one dared to contradict him.

†This could also be understood as: "If a sovereign whose conduct is contrary to reason fails in his enterprises, he benefits from the favor of Heaven, but if on the contrary he achieves his ambitions, he will be punished by Heaven." My interpretation is based on an analogous sequence pronounced by the famous statesman Fan Li in the "Yüeh's Discourse" section of the *Kuo-yu.*

top; he is right in each of his actions. The one who does not know how to retain his serenity when he rises to the top will lose the support of Heaven; the one whose actions are not right violates its decrees. Whoever kills populations that do not submit, massacres enemies that have surrendered, executes the innocent, will attract misfortune to himself: he will be punished fivefold if he punishes a guilty principality, he will be punished tenfold if he punishes an innocent principality.

A prince who does not know how to resist when the country is invaded, whose dissolute subjects think only of carving up the territories for their own personal profit, [will perish]; the one who, in wanting to lend aid to another, not only proves incapable of it but becomes the gateway to misfortune is the root of danger. The one whose glory rests on nothing solid will put his country in peril and will lose his possessions. Undertaking great works in summer is called going against the natural order. Heaven's punishment necessarily befalls the one who violates its prohibitions and flouts the natural order.

The Six Dangers are as follows: there is danger when the crown prince replaces the father, danger when the dignitaries replace the sovereign, danger when the strategists are not attached to you, danger when promotions and demotions are inspired by the other lords, danger when the prince finds himself isolated because of conspiracies within his circle, danger when the sovereign's relatives conspire and thwart his orders. If the sovereign does not manage to rid himself [of] the [Six] Dangers, misfortune will sweep down on him.

The Three Injustices are as follows: there is injustice first when one executes the sages; there is injustice second when one puts to death enemies who have surrendered; there is injustice third when one punishes those guilty of no crime. Those are the Three Injustices.

Let us move on now to the Three Confinements.

> When the women of the women's quarters rise above the sovereign and the way of the throne is blocked, when the court dignitaries dominate and the sovereign's hands are tied; especially when the women and the dignitaries together have preeminence and the sovereign is totally isolated: in such a case, the country will be unable to solidly maintain its defenses and win pitched battles. This is the first confinement.
>
> When the internal commands the external, there is confusion, when the external commands the internal, there is [. . .], when the external and the internal fight for preeminence, the country's security finds itself threatened. This is the second confinement.
>
> When just one man claims the sovereign's authority, it is said that he intercepts his light; if the sovereign finds himself surrounded internally and externally, he is then a prisoner twofold; especially when the internal and external unite and become one against the sovereign, the country changes hands. This is the third confinement.

What are the Three Evils? The first consists of loving the instruments of death, the second of developing warlike powers, the third of giving free rein to passions. Those are the Three Evils.

Whoever covets the empire's riches will turn the whole empire against him; whoever covets a country's riches will turn the whole country against him. Betraying one's allies, that is what I call not respecting one's engagements; renouncing a punitive expedition against a guilty principality because it has made you glowing promises, that is what I call not applying the punishments; killing one's father or assassinating one's brother, expelling one's sons or one's juniors, that is what I call being a troublemaker; violating the treaties signed with other princes, that is what I call attracting resentment. The sovereign who is guilty of these things will perish; [the one who inflicts just punishment upon him] will flourish.

Summary of the Great Principles

It is in the natural order that the civil takes precedence over the military; it is in the power of things that the four seasons succeed one another in an orderly fashion; it is in the law of the universe that the movements of the sun, the moon, and the constellations obey numerical calculations. Three seasons for growth and fruitfulness, one season for punishment and death: such is the course of things within the universe.* The four seasons each arrive in its own time, and their cycle knows neither trouble nor deviance. They are ruled by an immutable law that means there are [. . .] accession then decline, birth then death. The seasons replace one another in a regular cycle; once completed, it begins anew.

Giving a rational course to human affairs consists of proceeding in such a way that the normal and the aberrant each have their assigned place. The one whose exploits exceed the boundaries set by Heaven will be punished; the one whose achievements do not attain the standard set by Heaven will

---

*The same idea is expressed in the tenth chapter of the *Ho Kuan Tzu*.

live in obscurity and without renown. Only the one whose works are in accord with Heaven will know glory. Such is the rational course of human affairs.

Whoever follows the natural inclination lives, whoever is in accord with the rational order achieves, whoever opposes it perishes, [whoever neglects it is without renown]; when one turns his back on the natural course of things, the country is deprived of a master; in a country without a master, the normal collides with the aberrant so that the base is attacked, the structure brought down, the worst disorder reigns among living beings, and the principality is threatened with ruin. Even if it benefits from the aid of Heaven, it cannot avoid losing a share of its provinces and passing into other hands.*

Whoever does not conform to the rhythm of the seasons, whoever does not conserve the strength of his people will see the yearly cycle completed without a harvest. Whoever lets those who must perish live and makes those who deserve to live perish develops principles contrary to the natural order; if he is not punished by men, he will be punished by Heaven.

When the first manifestations of deviant behavior appear, be very careful not to intervene prematurely. Let the other one draw the wrath of Heaven down upon himself.† Those with political

---

*This could be understood in two ways. Either: "But if the country benefits from the aid of Heaven, the disaster will be limited to the loss of a few provinces and a change of sovereign," or "Having thus attracted Heaven's [punishment], the country will lose a share of its provinces and will change hands."

†There is a similar passage in the chapter called "Positional Advantage" in the *Kuan Tzu,* where the idea is further developed: "When the signs of deviant behavior first appear, and Heaven and Earth have not yet dealt ruthlessly with it, if you launch a punitive expedition prematurely, the operation risks failure and this error exposes you to punishment."

aims are used to seizing the moment when the event occurs. They scrutinize forms and names; forms and names once established, they draw the dividing line between the normal and the aberrant, between life and death, between endurance and extinction, between rise and fall. Then assessing the facts according to the standard of the immutable laws of the universe, they determine where to find happiness and misfortune, life and death, endurance and extinction, ascension and decline. That is the reason why their movements are always appropriate and why they never omit any factors from their evaluations. They reinforce the Son of Heaven on his throne, establish the Three Dukes in their offices, and ensure that the empire submits to their civilizing influence. That is what is called possessing the art of politics.

Standards and Names

The Way is the source of Mind,* the Mind is what confines itself within the rule even while manifesting itself outside the rule.†

---

*The Chinese term translated by "Mind" is *shan-ming,* a binomial formed from two characters, one of which means "god," "divine," "efficacious," and the second "luminous," "clear-sighted," "enlightened." Thus the expression sometimes forms an indissoluble whole, sometimes the product of two distinct though interdependent components. *Shan-ming* denotes both the faculties of the mind, capable of understanding and perceiving, and the primal entities *shan,* "efficiency," and *ming,* "luminosity," that precede the appearance of yin and yang and follow the formation of Heaven and Earth. But *shan* and *ming* also sometimes refer to the dual quality of the sovereign who is *shan,* hidden from the sight of others, secret, impenetrable, invisible as a mind, but at the same time is penetrating, *ming,* and sees everything that takes place around him.

†The word *chien,* translated here as "manifesting itself," could be understood as "to see," its primary meaning. It would thus have to be translated as "even in perceiving what is outside the rule," as Leo S. Chang and Yu Feng do in their English version.

Installed within the rule, it is forthright without speaking; manifested outside the rule, it speaks without varying; installed within the rule, immobile, it cannot be disturbed; manifested outside the rule, it moves without being altered. Unable to be disturbed when immobile or altered when moving, it is called divine; indeed Mind provides the standard of all knowledge.

Arising from the Earth, it is an entity that extends beyond Heaven and no one can perceive its form. Filling everything, it encompasses all the space between Heaven and Earth, without anyone knowing its name. It is because no one can know it that evil exists in the universe; from this arise all sorts of matters in a chaotic flow, so much so that there are inappropriate punishments, that misfortunes befall us, that we spare those who should perish and kill those who deserve to live, that we undermine our own foundations, cut ourselves off from our relatives, attack our allies [. . .], to end by wasting the country in blood and fire and earning a death without glory.

Any impatient impetuousness is contrary to enterprises, displays of self-satisfaction and arrogance are contrary to life,* stimulating the growth of beings through artificial means causes their premature death. In these three circumstances, acting outside of the rules in the hope of vain success, not only will one fail, but moreover, one will perish [. . .]. Whoever is strong and presents himself as weak will live, whoever is weak and presents himself as strong will perish by the sword.

---

*These two phrases can be interpreted many ways, according to the way the written forms of certain characters in the manuscript are corrected. It could be understood equally as: "Being like water and fire is contrary to enterprises; straightening instead of bending is contrary to nature."

Whoever is doubly weak will experience good fortune, whoever is doubly strong will be destroyed.

By *yes* you mark agreement, by *no* refusal. When *yes* and *no* are not worthy of faith, intelligence goes astray. But as soon as *yes* and *no* are worthy of faith, we evolve within the rule.

When some matter arises, I examine the names. Once the names are [established], through them I go back to what conforms to the standard. Whoever is in the right is rewarded; whoever is in the wrong suffers misfortune. It is up to the law to decide between true and false. Empty, calm, devoting all my attention and applying the law, I match the contracts; I examine and compare standards and names from all angles. That is what is called judging according to the reason of things. Freed of all prejudice, only the one who is impartial will not be abused and will know how to take vigorous action.

When experts knowledgeable in the Tao examine matters, they consider the correct way, judge according to the standard, separate the wheat from the chaff, and discover all the ins and outs. They use the denominations as a basis for examination in the light of the standard.* The name of things is expressed by the word; as soon as reality and the word are in perfect accord, misfortune and happiness, dismissal and promotion are like the shadow attached to the form, like the echo that responds to the voice, like the weight discovered on the tray of the scales. That is why only the possessors of the Way can

---

*The whole passage sounds legalist and recalls sequences from *Han Fei Tzu,* especially the fifth and eighth chapters, "The Way of the Master" and "Doctrinal Manifesto," among others.

judge things with serenity and impartiality. They separate [the wheat from the chaff] and arrive at the essence of names and standards.

When a principality accrues all the factors of disorder internally, and powers are balanced unfavorably toward it externally, it will be punished; when signs of an imminent demise are manifested within and operations fail from without, it will be destroyed. The sovereign who rebels against the course of things and who, filled with arrogance, does not know when to stop is doomed. A country that, profiting from its neighbor's weakness, attacks it and fails in its enterprise is favored by Heaven; had it succeeded, it would have suffered an inglorious end.

[Dissolute behavior] seriously impedes the course of things; the sovereign who adopts such an attitude and puts it into practice will expose his principality and himself to misfortune. No country can escape ruin when it is the battlefield of two rebel forces joined to produce calamities.

CANON II

THE GREAT CANONICAL RULES*

Instituting the Mandate

Because long ago the Yellow Ancestor† was truly the first to give the place of honor to faith in the given word, he set himself up as a model. He was a four-sided square surrounding a single heart, in such a way that the four sides radiated from the center. The front was divided into three, the back as well; three on the left and three on the right. And occupying the

---

*Chinese scholars interpret this title in various ways. Some read it as "The Ten Great Rules" (*Shih-ta ching*), others as "The Sixteen Rules" (*Shih-liu ching*), since the characters *liu* (six) and *ta* (great) are close graphically and can easily be confused. Nevertheless, there are neither ten nor sixteen rules, but fourteen of them. The great contemporary scholar Li Xueqin proposed an ingenious solution originating in a different division of the characters that appear at the end of the section. According to him, "*Shih-ta*" designates the title of the last subsection that concludes the second part and means "The Ten Great (Maxims)," so the true title of this section would thus be simply "*Ching*," "The Canons." Unfortunately, the scholar has to divide the last paragraph in a very arbitrary way to arrive at ten maxims.

†Another name for the Yellow Emperor, the first of the five primordial sovereigns; instituting the sovereignty, he rules the center and has the Earth for his emblem.

seat of power by wandering over the trinity, he was able to be the patriarch of the empire:*

> I receive the mandate from Heaven, I strengthen my position on Earth and achieve my renown among men. I alone, the only Man, can aid Heaven. Thus I establish the kings, I establish the three dukes, I establish the princes and the ministers. I calculate the days, count the lunar months, and establish the calculations for the years in order to harmonize the progress of the sun and the moon. Vast and profuse as the Earth, my light is in the image of Heaven.
>
> I fear Heaven, I love Earth and cherish the people [. . .] dismissing those who do not have the mandate, I retain emptiness and authenticity. I fear Heaven, I love Earth and cherish the people. I establish those who have the mandate, I retain emptiness and authenticity.
>
> I love the people and the people do not abandon me, I

---

*What is described here is the *Ming-t'ang,* the "Palace of Lights." Simultaneously the royal palace, seat of the government, and home of the calendar, it belongs more to the utopian world than to reality, or rather, it is the manifestation of a ritualistic utopia in architectural form. (For the meaning of the passage, refer to the section of the introduction titled "The Emptiness of the Sovereign and the Asceticism of the Yellow Emperor.") Nevertheless, another interpretation is possible, which does not, in fact, contradict the one we give; it is simply located on a different plane, in reference to the purpose of the architectural design: "He looked in the four directions at once, even as he devoted himself to concentrating his mind. That is how he could project himself into the four directions from the center, investigating [the word *san* means both "three" and "to examine," "to investigate"] close up those who were in front, investigating close up those who were in back, investigating close up those who were to the left, investigating close up those who were to the right. And even once he had climbed the steps of the throne, he continued to investigate."

love the Earth and the Earth is not barren. I receive the people [. . .] death. My position is not [. . .]. Because I know how to cherish those near to me and promote the sages, without distributing my wealth, the people will flock to me.

Inspection

The Yellow Emperor ordered Power of the Pen* to go incognito among the princes of the four directions in order to determine if their morals were not always good. This is how Power of the Pen reflected the view offered him: black was black, white was white. As to the Earth, [he reflected its landscapes: cheerful, he was cheerful, ungrateful†], he was ungrateful. He was like a mirror sending back the image of the man: resting, he was at rest, moving, he was in motion. Once Power of the Pen had proclaimed the Rules and claimed the Great Summit [. . .].

Power of the Pen said:

"Once Heaven and Earth formed, humanity appeared without the criteria of good and evil being established, without vice and virtue receiving their proper due, neither the times of

---

*"Power of the Pen," or Li Mo, often spelled differently, is one of the Yellow Emperor's chief ministers. The words *li* (strength) and *mo* (ink) have a phonetic value in his name; to the extent that the Yellow Emperor could institute the state administration thanks to the invention of writing by his minister Ts'an Chieh, and that Li Mo symbolizes the faithful retranscription of reality in this passage, it seems that the choice of these characters is not insignificant.

†Completed according to the suggestions of translators Leo S. Chang and Yu Feng.

activity or rest had been instituted, nor the status of before and after defined. Now today I would like to establish the frameworks of good and evil, [give vice and virtue their proper due, institute the times of activity and rest, and define the status of before and after], in order to be the regulator of the empire. How then to draw inspiration from the phases of activity and rest indicated by Heaven in order to rein in the people?"

The Yellow Emperor replied:

"Profuse [. . .] and gathered into a ball, there was neither light nor darkness, yin and yang did not yet exist; yin and yang not being condensed, it was impossible to assign names to things. Then primordial chaos split up. From its division were born yin and yang, which, separating in their turn, produced the four seasons. [. . .] follows in order that it serves as rule. They made the luminous laws on the model of the stars, even while knowing how to resort to secret ways when action required it, following the example of the stars eclipsing their light.* They applied the law and conformed [. . .] the male and the female.

"The male and female seek one another, prompting the encounter of hard and soft; hard and soft complementing

---

*This is undoubtedly an allusion to the two chief tools of legalist domination, the law (*fa*) and the art of manipulation (*shu*). Universal, public, and impartial, the law is the instrument by which the state administration controls the population; secret, private, and occasional, political (or police) art is the means by which the sovereign ensures for himself the faithfulness of the members of the State system. Just as the stars have two aspects, one visible, one hidden, the government has two faces: apparent and secret. This could also be understood as a matter of rewards (in the limelight) and punishments (done discreetly). In another passage, daytime, yang, and rewards are opposed to nighttime, yin, and punishments.

one another, male and female give life. They mate below on Earth; they mate above in Heaven. Whoever has grasped the mystery of Heaven, the moment [. . .], under the effect of the impulses issuing from Earth, seeds begin to sprout and shoots to grow. Heaven favors their growth by conforming to their needs; otherwise nothing would be produced. Living beings would perish if they were not cherished. The survival of the people depends on the food and care provided them. Without mating and descendants, who would look after the territory? Without food or men, who would provide for the worship of Heaven?

"[That is how] the sovereign, extending his generosity at the time of yin's greatest fullness, [stimulating at the opportune time] the people's labor, thus ensures his survival. At the time of yang's greatest fullness, the sovereign prepares to apply punishments. When yin grows to the point that the nights have become longer than the days, the impulses are blocked, and the Earth is in labor, encounters favoring the perpetuation of the species take place. That is why, to keep the people on the right path, there is no need to rein them in; it is enough to conform to the natural system of gifts and punishments. Spring and summer are the seasons of benefits, autumn and winter the seasons of punishments. Precedence is given to rewards over punishments in order to further the growth of life.

"Once clans have formed, conflicts break out between those with equal strength. And it is vain to hope to ensure order as long as they continue. Now, there is no better tool for quelling them than the system of rewards and punishments. They must be brilliant as the sun and the moon that shine in turn on high, the one lighting up at the required time, the other waxing and [waning] in a regular cycle.

"Generally, in relationships with the people, be careful not to aggravate men; in military operations, be careful not to aggravate yang; in the labors of the field, be careful not to exhaust yin. Whoever exhausts yin wears out the Earth, whoever aggravates yang loses all splendor; where men are aggravated the clash of weapons rings out. The master of men sees to it that the people have three seasons to take delight in, thus he does not disturb the people in their work, nor does he thwart the cycle of the seasons. The grain grows in abundance; the people grow and multiply. Princes and ministers, superiors and subordinates devote themselves to answering their reciprocal aspirations and Heaven, responding to their desires, furthers their enterprises.

"Obeying Heaven is to conform to the rhythm of the seasons so as to further the labors of the field, and to give precedence to rewards over punishments. If, when the season is in its fullness, activities are restricted, a return of yin is produced and the impulses of the Earth regather. If one proceeds with the execution of punishments at the time of the proclamation of seasonal regulations, the hibernating insects will remain hidden under the Earth, snow and ice will begin to fall again, the millet will shrivel up, and all sorts of calamities will strike; under these circumstances, no enterprise can be conducted successfully.

"If, when the period is in its downturn, one devotes oneself to the activities of the high season, a return of yang is produced and the impulses of the Earth cannot regather; if one postpones the execution of punishments at the time of the proclamation of seasonal regulations, the hibernating insects will make their songs heard, the plants begin to grow again; to want to make yang revive when its cycle is complete is to repeat a season twice without obtaining any additional splendor; in such circumstances, no enterprise will be able to succeed.

"When one conforms fully to Heaven's mode of action, on Earth, beings will be complete. To watch that goods circulate and that beings are produced is the task of the sage. The sage does not value cleverness; he is content to follow the cyclical movement of time. He is concerned with cherishing the people and distributing his blessings to them; that is why he acts in the manner of Heaven. Full of rectitude, he watches for the moment assigned by Heaven; immobile, he awaits the support of men, he does not lighten the punishments decided by Heaven, he does not neglect his engagements, he adheres to the moment and he rules in accordance with Heaven. Because he knows that by not ruling when circumstances require, one greatly risks suffering the wrath of Heaven."

The Five Regulations

The Yellow Emperor asked Yen Jan:*

"I want to extend the Five Regulations to the empire, where to begin, or end?"

Yen Jan responded:

"Begin with your own body. Once your heart of hearts is regulated, that will reflect on the exterior. Once interior and exterior are in accord, you can put the affairs of the empire in order."

---

*Another of the Yellow Emperor's ministers.

The Yellow Emperor asked again:

"If my soul is regulated and nevertheless the country is still plagued with troubles, what do I do?"

Yen Jan answered:

"That is because, however regulated your soul and well governed the exterior, you have not known how to establish [the rules and laws] at all. If you hold the level in your right hand, and the compass in your left, would you have to worry about the empire? If men and women were perfectly united with their master, what thought would you give the realm? If the Five Regulations were at work in the nation, you would have control of the Five Clarities.* If the compass and the level were held solidly in your right and left hands, you could await the opposing army resolutely."

The Yellow Emperor asked:

"How do I do this if I do not know myself?"

"If you do not know yourself," answered the minister,

---

*What these Five Regulations (*wu-cheng*) and Five Clarities are is not clear. Chinese scholars who have checked the retranscription and editing of the manuscripts refer to a passage in the eighth chapter of the *Ho Kuan Tzu*, "Embracing Totality," where an equivalent expression appears: "Heaven and Earth, yin and yang have their counterparts in the human body. Putting to work the Five Types of Government (*wu-cheng*) falls under the responsibility of the Five Brilliances (*wu-ming*)." The most recent critical edition of the *Ho Kuan Tzu* also emphasizes the relationship of these two passages and thus likens the Five Regulations and the Five Clarities of *The Four Canons* with the Five Regulators and the Five Brilliances of the *Ho Kuan Tzu*. But lexical similarities are often deceptive: according to the text, it appears that the five kinds of regulators correspond to five forms of mutually exclusive regulations, placed under the patronage of a kind of sovereign master of denominations (*ming*, "brilliance," sometimes equivalent to *ming*, "name," through phonic substitution). Whereas, according to the context, in the "then leave the world in order to conduct an examination of your consciousness. When that is done, you will know how to display modesty."

The Yellow Emperor asked:

"What must I do to display modesty?"

The minister answered:

"Those who are moved by similar principles act in an identical fashion, those who obey opposing principles act in opposing fashions. Today if war raged in the empire, would you know, at the right moment, to beware of aggressiveness?"

The emperor asked:

"How am I to beware of it?"

The minister replied:

"Anger arises from the blood and the breath; aggressiveness expresses itself through the skin. If one does not release one's anger, it forms abscesses by accumulating. If you are ready to

---

dialogue between the Yellow Emperor and his minister, it's a question not of instituting different regulations sponsored by different kinds of sovereigns, but rather of five kinds of concomitant regulations. In fact, the expression *wu-cheng* refers to all kinds of realities: in the third chapter of the same *Ho Kuan Tzu,* "Nocturnal Action," for example, it denotes the Five Planets. Again in the *Ho Kuan Tzu,* just before the mention of five political regimes (*wu-cheng*—though the words *cheng,* "regulation" and *cheng,* "political regime," homophones, are principally distinguished graphically, they are very often written interchangeably!), comes the mention of the regulators, *cheng,* five in number, which ensure control of the five kinds of entities: "Yin and yang are the regulator (*cheng*) of the breaths, Heaven and Earth are those respectively of the mind and of matter, the sage himself of efficiency, the Law, that of the seasons." These could very well be the Five Brilliances Yen Jan alludes to: yin-yang, Heaven, Earth, sage, Law.

abandon the Four Emotions,* like a pile of dry bones,† you will never give in to aggressiveness."

Upon that, the Yellow Emperor abandoned the affairs of the empire and took refuge on Distant View Mountain, where he remained meditating for three years in order to find himself again.

With wars raging more fiercely than ever, Yan Jen went to find him. He said:

"Now you are ready. Even if the conflicts are disastrous,‡ if you refuse to fight, you will never achieve anything. Isn't this the moment?"

The Yellow Emperor seized his halberd, incited his army, beat the drum, and took on Ch'e-yu.§ He vanquished him and had an oath engraved. The words of it were as follows:

"Whoever rebels against justice and the seasonal ordi-

---

*The Chinese text is content with just "the Four," which the text editors and translators in turn have understood to be the blood, the breath, the fat, and the skin (the binomial expression *chih-lu* is translated by the single term "skin" here), but that does not make a lot of sense. Rather, the sovereign is prevented from governing by the Four Emotions discussed in the "*Ch'u-yüan*" chapter of the *Kuan Tzu*: joy, anger, pleasure, and disgust. Let us note that very similar lists are found in the "*Pai-hsin*" and "*Nei-yeh*" chapters of the same book.

†This expression belongs to the vocabulary of ecstatic Taoism and serves to designate the appearance of the one who, over the course of mystical wanderings, is separated from his ego. The *Chuang Tzu* repeatedly uses similar phrases, such as "body like dry wood" and "heart like extinguished cinders," to depict the physical state rendered by this regime of the consciousness.

‡This phrase is repeated in section 31 of the *Lao Tzu* and cited time and again by all the treatises on strategic arts.

§Ch'e-yu is an important figure in ancient Chinese mythology; he was supposed to have invented weapons. He is sometimes described as a rebel minister of the Yellow Emperor.

nances will suffer the punishment inflicted upon Ch'e-yu! Whoever rebels against his master will perish under the blows of the law!"

Child of Truth

The Yellow Emperor questioned his Four Aides:

"Here I am, the only Man, finding myself at the head of the whole empire. How must I go about it if I want to provide for its upkeep and keep it on the right path, distributing goods fairly and making equality rule?"

Child of Truth answered:*

"There is no equity without inquiry,† nor any rectitude

---

*Child of Truth, *Kuo t'ung* in Chinese, is one of the "Four Aides," *szu-fu,* ministers, mentioned above. He does not appear elsewhere. *Kuo,* translated as "truth" here, also means "result," "perseverance." Thus in the *Lao Tzu,* section 30, the word appears repeatedly to describe the great strategist who does not let himself be carried away by his successes (*kuo*). So this could be translated "Child Who Sees Things Through." The term *t'ung* was not chosen by chance; mediums are called *ch'i-t'ung,* "children of the divining rod," or more simply *t'ung-tzu,* "small boys." All mystical asceticism involves a regression, and it is closely associated with childhood. In chapter 14 of the *Chuang Tzu,* the Yellow Emperor loses his way in the country while he is searching for the sage T'ai-wei, and he is instructed in the art of governing by a young shepherd whom one suspects is none other than the primordial form of T'ai-wei and the human impersonation of the Tao.

†The Chinese word is *hsien,* which means "steep," "unequal," or "severity of the law," but here, I think, it is a matter of a phonic borrowing (attested in the *I Ching*) for *chien,* which means "to examine," "to inquire," "to verify," and is only distinguished from *hsien* by the substitution of the radical for "wood" with the radical for "mounds." The word *hsien* corresponds closely to *kan,* "to examine," and the two parts of the sentence are parallel. By retaining the first meaning of *hsien,* it could be understood also as "It is through contrasts that equality is ensured, it is through surveillance that rectitude is maintained," but then the parallelism breaks down.

without examination. Raising one's eyes toward Heaven, which stretches above, lowering one's eyes to Earth, which extends below, one draws from them the standards that must govern relationships between men and women. Heaven has its intangible trunks, Earth its immutable laws, it unites [. . .] constant; light and dark alternate, yin and yang take turns. Plain and mountain, shadow and light, aridity and fertility give to the Earth their contrasts.

"In rest, Earth possesses nurturing virtue; in movement, Heaven directs the denominations. Movement and rest complement one another; rewards and punishments complete one another; when the two principles each receive their name, their collaboration is fruitful. Yin and yang produce all the beings from which the transformations are born. Thus, if for some it is already too much to perform a single task, others can accomplish a hundred of them without effort. Each man has his talent as each thing has its form. Whoever knows how to put it to good use succeeds."

The Yellow Emperor said:

"Men draw their existence from Heaven and are dependent on Earth for their food. Heaven is their father and Earth their mother. Now since my intention is to provide for the upkeep of the people and keep them on the right path, to distribute goods to them fairly and make equality rule, through whose intercession must I begin?"

His advisor answered:

"It is through inquiries that you will ensure the just distribution of goods; and through surveillance that you will keep the people on the right path. The distinction between base and noble must be established and the hierarchy between poor and rich set in place. Models instituted by precursors must be followed* by posterity. Thus I am ready to get under way."

Child of Truth, dressed in rags, a cracked jar on his back, left on his adventure, begging for his bread throughout the empire. He traveled among the princes of the four directions and experienced the most extreme poverty and baseness.

Quelling Disturbances

Power of the Pen asked:

"[. . .] full of pride [. . .] and hatched plots [. . .] Great Thunder† [. . .] how to do?"

Standard of Mount T'ai‡ answered:

"Do not be afraid. Heaven follows a steady, regular course; the sun and the moon never stop and, in a bubbling, radiant flow, creation pours out its manna over the empire without pause or rest.

"Since man's nature is finite, he has insatiable desires. They will [quickly] lead him to ruin. Opulence will make him [heedless], [heedlessness] will lead him to his end; gifts will be

---

*I have adopted Yu Mingguang's interpretation that considers the word *yüan*, "to break," as a phonic borrowing for the homophone *yüan*, "to follow." Without adopting his suggestion, the meaning would be exactly the opposite.

†Grandson of the Yellow Emperor, second on the list of the Five Emperors, he is better known by the name of Shuan-hsiu.

‡The name of one of the Yellow Emperor's advising ministers who is mentioned in many legendary accounts, T'ai-shan chih-chi or T'ai-shan chi in Chinese. Yu Mingguang thinks that here it is used as another name for the Yellow Emperor. However, in all the passages where the emperor appears, he always adopts the stance of the student facing his masters—sticking to an "I do not dare" and "I am unable" mode, which is not at all the case here.

harmful to him, sums of money will incite him to wastefulness, idleness will provoke [indolence]. Torment him, prompt his fear, and he will be cornered, then you can to grab hold of him and beat him to a pulp. Set about raising him up, and once at the top, push him down so that he can never recover from his fall. Come on, don't worry, we can hurl him into the pit before he even has time to be sorry!"

Power of the Pen objected:

"We had already done battle over sixty times before Great Thunder even reached adulthood. [Having insatiable desires and so on . . .] isn't that called benefiting from Heaven's aid? Benefiting from Heaven's aid and not making military preparations, isn't that exposing oneself to Heaven and Earth no longer acting as one?* What do you think of that?"

Standard of Mount T'ai:

"Do not speak of Heaven's aid! I am going to stage preparations against him. I count favoring his enterprises, exciting his ambitions, increasing his power, by handing over to him the lands of Tai.† Not another word about that! It is enough that the sovereign be upright and hold to the One, while his subordinates display calm. The sovereign can count on the opportunity Heaven will surely provide him because of his uprightness; the subordinates can count on the support their

---

*I interpret this sentence according to the manuscript editors' correction by which the character *kuan,* "to watch over," "function," is a transcription error, the character being a graphic variant for *ti,* "Earth," twice represented. The expression might be a periphrasis meaning that, without sufficient precautions, the subject (Earth) risks elevating itself to the rank of Heaven (the sovereign), so that they will be confused.

†This translation is conjectural. Very diverse interpretations have been proposed.

calmness will ensure for them among the people. Heaven and Earth provide the model for designations. [. . .] are produced by themselves and submit to celestial punishments. Heaven never punishes wrongly; good and evil are perfectly defined.

"Do not be afraid if you have not [made] military preparations; he has only just revealed his seditious intentions. First we will let him give free rein to his excesses, then we will crush him. We will appoint another minister* who will take his place among the Six Advisors and who will be entirely devoted to us. When the situation is ripe, it will not be necessary to reveal ourselves, only to let the trap shut by itself. On the one hand, I will act according to the lesson I have been able to draw from past events; on the other, I will wait to see the new tricks he will surely develop to adapt to my strategy. Knowing simultaneously how to take the initiative and how to respond to the adversary's movements is to possess a miraculous art, worthy of Heaven and Earth. And moreover, since there will inevitably be uprisings and killings among his people, I will make sure that he brings about his own downfall."

When war was raging, Standard of Mount T'ai said: "It is time." Then the Yellow Emperor brandished his halberd, deployed his arm, met Ch'e-yu, and vanquished him. He skinned him and made a target for his soldiers; the one who drew the most arrows by the end was rewarded. He scalped him and hung his hair in Heaven, which is what we now call Ch'e-yu's Banner. He inflated his stomach like a balloon and

---

*Even though he is not expressly named, this must be Ch'e-yu, who is the Yellow Emperor's minister in certain traditions, the one related by the *Kuan Tzu* among them.

gave it to his men to kick; the one who took the most shots at it by the end was rewarded. He had his flesh and bones macerated, threw them into brine, and gave them to the whole empire to taste.*

His Highness the Emperor then issued a prohibition in which it was said:

"No one must disobey my edicts, no one must spill my brine, no one must disturb my people, no one must block my road. Whoever breaks my rules, spills my brine, disturbs my people, blocks my road, opposes justice and acts against the seasonal regulations, acts badly, exceeds the norms and loses the sense of proportion, changes laws to his own liking, let all those who would wish to act in such ways know that before they are able to raise an army, his Highness the Emperor will make them suffer the fate of the minister of public works, Ch'e-yu! I will bend their backs until I make them [lick their behinds].† And neither dead nor alive, they will become the pillar of earth!"‡

---

*This describes a ritual punishment. Many texts allude to the practice of chopping up the guilty party's body, marinating it in brine, and selling it in jars at the marketplaces to serve as a warning to the people.

†The meaning of this expression is not clear and gives rise to all sorts of conjectures.

‡The expression "neither dead nor alive" goes back to a shamanic context. In the sixth chapter of the *Chuang Tzu,* thanks to a dialogue between an immortal (the Lady who goes all alone) and an adept, the author teaches us that one of the stages of regression leading to enlightenment is "the domain where there is neither life nor death." Similarly, the "pillar of earth" certainly evokes ritual events. During the Taoist ceremony for purifying sacred ground, a dance takes place miming the struggle between the Taoist master and an evil demon. Vanquished by the master, the troublemaker becomes a beneficent protector when his mask is ripped off and placed in a pail full of rice in the northeast corner, called "the demons' door," and the exorcist plunges in his sword to fix him there for good.

The emperor spoke again:

"Treasure my proper denominations, do not let my just punishments fall into oblivion, so that they may instruct posterity!"

Fighting between Clans

The Emperor Great Thunder asked Power of the Pen:

"After Heaven and Earth were formed, the dark-haired people appeared; but even today no one conforms to the virtue of Heaven, each conspires to ruin the other. That distresses me. How do I remedy it?"

Power of the Pen:

"Do not distress yourself; it is in the order of things. It is natural that once the universe was formed, living beings would struggle against one another. Of course, war is disastrous, but whoever refuses to take up arms achieves nothing. Whoever follows Heaven flourishes, whoever opposes it perishes. Take care not to go against the natural operation of things and you will remain master of your possessions. Once the universe was formed, the dark-haired people appeared. Once the people formed into clans, conflict struck between those of equal strength. It is vain to hope to establish order as long as there is no end to it.

"Now there is no better tool for quieting dissension than the system of rewards and punishments. They must be luminous as the sun and moon that rise to the heights by turn and shine advisedly, and that would be harbingers of disaster if they did not reach their highest point at the required time. Heaven's blessings are radiant, but they could not function without punishments; its punishments are imposing, but they would cause ruin without blessings. The difference between normal and aberrant becomes clear thanks to the mutual support that rewards and punishments offer one another.

"Punishments are night, rewards are day, punishments are yin in nature, rewards yang, punishments are discreet, rewards displayed. What is radiant must serve the law, but some modes of action must be secret. Only by penetrating the pendulum's movement within the heavenly mechanism can one grasp that the light always has its share of darkness.

"Heaven's movements prompt reversals among men, which is why those attacked turn into the attackers. The one whose movements are always in accord with the circumstances will win the support of Heaven and Earth. Whoever fights without pause or respite, and whoever does not know to remain at rest when the circumstances demand it, will never bring peace to his country. But the one who does not know to take the initiative when the moment to act arrives, by virtue of the swing of Heaven's pendulum, leaves the role of assailant to his enemy. Thus, to summarize, Heaven lends its support to the one who knows to act at the right moment; the one who acts out of rhythm, Heaven and Earth will ravage.

"It is in the order of things that heat and cold, dry and humid cannot coexist, neither can yin and yang, hard and soft be concurrent. The two principles nurture each other, just as the seasons mutually complete one another. When the people conform to the laws in times of peace and when they obey orders in times of war, the prince will succeed in all his undertakings without trying. But where no constant principle in conducting human affairs is adopted, where the limits are exceeded and a sense of proportion is lost, where habits and customs are changed for no reason, where rewards are paltry and punishments arbitrary, where laws are not followed in time of peace nor orders obeyed in times of war, there is hardly any doubt that misfortune will strike the prince."

The Attitude of the Hen and the Rooster

The emperor examined at depth the laws regarding harmful and good in order to distinguish between the attitudes of the rooster and the hen, from which ensue bad and good fortune. Arrogance and haughtiness: that is the masculine attitude; moderation and restraint: female behavior. Whoever plays the rooster squanders, whoever plays the hen saves. To acquire through the rooster's attitude does not ensure one's fortune, to lose through the hen's conduct earns one dividends. Repeated success by the rooster redoubles misfortunes, worries giving way to failures leading finally to ruin. Repeated failure by the hen accrues gains. Be vigilant in respecting this rule and the profits are extreme.

All misfortune results because the one who advances suffers in relationship to the one who stays in retreat. Through the attitude of the hen, one can advance without experiencing misfortune. Through the masculine attitude, one experiences setbacks even staying in retreat. Thus, through the first, one always knows success, through the second, one always knows defeat. Whoever adopts masculine behavior puts his days in danger; the man of much will be shaken and the man of little will be lost. The one who conforms to it will not be able to hold his positions and his undertakings will fail, he will be defeated in battles, he will not live long, his descendants will not be prosperous; it is a disastrous attitude, one squanders his power.

But the one who knows how to model himself on female behavior realizes profits; rich, he becomes richer, poor, he achieves ease; he preserves what he defends and succeeds in his undertakings, obtains what he covets and emerges victorious from his battles; he enjoys longevity and has many descendants; this is good conduct, it makes virtue shine. Through accumulated virtue one is raised, through repeated misfortune one is ruined. It is enough to observe what each accumulates to have the key to his fate.

The Face of War

If the army does not take Heaven for its model, it cannot be mobilized; if it does not take Earth for a model, it cannot be deployed; if the men in it are not controlled by punishments, it cannot form its ranks. [That is why one must know how to combine the three moments. Man proposes],* Heaven and Earth dispose, the sage relies on them, and thus perfects. The secret of his successes: he makes the moment his servant. Taking advantage of the circumstances and seizing the opportunity, he accomplishes things once and for all. The sage does not defer punishments nor renounce his obligations. He waits for the moment offered by Heaven and acts in conjunction with it. He knows the risk of being

---

*The first four missing characters are filled in here according to an undoubtedly parallel phrase that appears in the first section and the next four according to a similar passage in the *Kuo-yü*'s "Discourse of Yüeh."

swept into the maelstrom by refusing to act when the circumstances demand it.

Heaven can take as it can give; [it dispenses] misfortune [as it does happiness; whoever refuses to accept] its gifts will suffer its wrath. Where the three channels are interrupted,* the army cannot achieve victory; and if by chance it were victorious, it would hardly profit from its success; just the opposite, as misfortune would befall it. In an arbitrary country, those in charge come to a sad end, in a country that is not arbitrary, they enjoy happy days.

Sure of the strength of their multitudes, the seething, impetuous tides, they carry off victory after victory, under the very nose of the celestial summit. Alas, they put their country in danger, shaking the altars of their gods of the soils and the harvests, and finally their undertakings end in failure, because the gods do not accept the fruits of their success. Such is the great Law of Heaven.

Proven Laws

The Yellow Emperor asked Power of the Pen:

"The traitors hold their heads high; the flatterers and sophists use shrewdness, I am very much afraid because if I, the only Man who is in charge of the empire, cannot manage to restrain them through the laws, someone else will use the opportunity to put the empire to fire and the sword. Is there no system of proven law for returning the people to the right path?"

---

*The "three channels" are knowledge of the climatic risks, topographical characteristics, and the morale of the men.

Power of the Pen:

"Yes. In the past, once Heaven and Earth were formed, since they stayed in their places, there were correct names; since they were in harmony, the forms were produced. [. . .] they watched over the only Name. Continuing the work of Heaven above, they diffused it below over the whole expanse between the four seas. As far as I know, the system of proven laws current at that time was most succinct; it kept to a single sentence: 'Follow the names to cause a return to the One, and the people will follow the right path.'"

The Yellow Emperor:

"Must the world still be ruled by the One?"

Power of the Pen:

"Yes. In the dawn of time, majestic Heaven sent Phoenix over Earth, transmitting to him a single phrase. The Five Emperors were content to apply this maxim, and that is how they could define the respective positions of Heaven and Earth, rule the four seas, care for the masses, and control the administrators in their epochs. The slanderers were dismissed and the sages promoted, the five kinds of corruptors were expelled as well as the courtesans, and the rhetoricians silenced. Yes, truly, when one follows the names to return to the One, the people are brought back to the right path."

The Yellow Emperor:

"But is the One reduced simply to the One, or is it capable of expansion?"

Power of the Pen:

"The One is the essence of the Tao, how under such conditions would it be capable of expansion? [All errors] come from not knowing how to retain the One. The expansion of the One embraces Heaven and Earth* and its organization principle governs all that exists between the four seas. How can one go back to the completion of the ring of creation and distinguish near from far? Only the One keeps one from getting lost there. The One is the engine of all transformations; thanks to it, it is possible to know everything beginning from nothing. Between the four seas, above and below, from east to west and north to south, all things follow their own way. Nevertheless, one hundred words are reduced to one phrase, one thousand to one principle, ten thousand to a summary. The throng of beings passes through the same orifice.

"Thus, only the man who possesses rectitude is capable of controlling all that. Yes, it truly takes an upright man to apply the right rule in order to rectify the deviant. Possessing expanded knowledge thanks to a single principle, ridding the people of their ills and applying policy that benefits them, holding to the essential and retaining the One, being moved by the same forces as Heaven and Earth: all this allows one to know the causes of happiness and misfortune in the universe."

The Three Prohibitions

Heaven prohibits lapses in conduct, Earth prohibits neglect of work, the prince prohibits disobedience to orders. Government is close to perfection when the Three Prohibitions are

---

*Characters are corrected here according to parallel passages appearing in the *Kuan Tzu* chapters titled "The Art of the Mind" ("*Hsin-shu*") and "Inner Work" ("*Nei-yeh*"), as well as the first chapter of the *Huai Nan Tzu,* "The Source of the Tao" ("*Tao-yüan*"). Otherwise, it can be read as: "Understanding the One allows for an intimate knowledge of the universe."

respected. Defending land requires that elevations not be leveled nor depressions filled in, that flowerbeds not be barred and yards not be bothered, that working the fields not be prevented, that the people not be deprived of the light. Pursuing enterprises without rest, building without taking a break, heedlessly forging ahead all constitute harmful behavior.

Human conduct must reconcile gentleness and resolve. Neither one nor the other is sufficient by itself. Whoever proves inflexible and behaves like a tiger will become destitute; whoever proves indolent and abandons himself to pleasures will experience decline; whoever takes antiquity for a model and cherishes vain dreams will cut himself off from reality and perish; whoever is moved by the lure of profit and takes from those who have nearly nothing in order to build fine homes will end up in poverty. High above as Heaven is, its actions are felt here below and its influence extends over the nine continents. That is why when the princes and the dukes attend to proclaiming the laws, the people do what they must. Thus, the sun completes its unchanging course in Heaven, and men conform to it: if they go against it, their lives are cut short and they bring misfortune down upon themselves. Such is the course of things.

The Reason for Punitive Expeditions

There are various ways for a State to use the weapons stored in its arsenals. In the present epoch, the modes are three in number: opportunity, justice, anger. It is a war of opportunity when, discovering that [the enemy is experiencing] famine, that the country is too busy elsewhere to defend itself, that superiors and subordinates are not keeping to their places, one raises an army and inflicts just punishment. Even if one does not gain a great advantage, he does not expose himself to great harm.

It is a war in the name of justice when one quiets unrest and punishes tyranny or puts a sage on the throne in place of an incompetent. That is called a just war. The majority of an army's soldiers are ready to sacrifice their lives for a just war. That is why, in the case where one realm attacks the other princes in the empire, one country lining up ten thousand war carts [. . .] if it frequently takes the initiative in such operations, it can rarely follow them through, because without great perseverance, the army will turn back empty-handed.

When campaigns are led through anger, it is because the anger one feels cannot simply remain a state of rage, it needs to be translated into actions. But then it is necessary that no demands are made once the victory is won, because to annex a territory would be in deliberate violation of Heaven. It is acting counter to the Tao. Only wars conducted under the sway of necessity conform to the Tao. The prince who resolves to fight only under constraint will never be caught short. That is why one [. . .] to free, prohibits to stimulate. That is the way one comes and goes through the empire without letting himself be stopped.

Priority Methods

The sage necessarily acts in accord with Heaven and Earth; he conforms to the will of the people and obeys the desires of the gods. And since everyone, without exception, derives advantage from his action, he benefits from the nation's approval. Possessing a sense of duty consists of presenting oneself to the sovereign so that he can charge you with a responsibility and, when the sovereign agrees to use you, to bring lasting profits to altars of the gods of the soil and the harvests and let the people benefit from the advantages of long life.

But when the high dignitaries in their carriages gain the high road, the valiant find themselves reduced to poverty. The ordinary knight is the one from whom a single word profits a single individual and a knight of the realm one from whom it profits a State. When good men must humble themselves to find ways of introducing themselves, when they must use their intelligence to refute their adversaries and prove their authority for their advice to be followed, when they must live among the masses even while bearing the weight of their virtue, and must bend over backward awaiting the right moment, it is a miracle that the princes and the nobles can know of their talents.*

A great power is a State with vast territories and a large population at its disposal [. . .] that is what comes under luck,

---

*This could also be understood to mean "The good man, full of humility, follows the Way, he applies all his intelligence to penetrating arcane mysteries, he does himself violence to put it into practice, he lives among his peers, charged with this burden, and knows how to prove his suppleness by waiting for the right moment. It is good luck for a country that the nobility can have knowledge of such men." But then "luck" would have a positive connotation, whereas it has a negative one here; given that it is impossible for men of high virtue to reach sovereigns, the channels of power being blocked by schemers and flatterers, it is not only vain but dangerous to hope for salvation through so improbable an encounter. Also, it is not on men but on institutions that the sovereign must rely essentially. I interpret the passage in the light of certain chapters of the *Han Fei Tzu*, particularly the one titled "A Solitary's Rage."

whereas a king must never count on luck to ensure order in his States. To govern a country, there are priority methods that consist of knowing climatic factors above, ground advantages below, and human activities in the middle. Whoever is versed in the science of yin and yang [. . .]. Regulated designations bring order, improper designations disorder. Where designations are regulated, there will be no deviance; where they are improper, institutions will not endure.

The true Way never slackens. It opens in things large and small. It is as suitable to a simple nobody as to a country. Thanks to it, an individual succeeds in his enterprises; thanks to it, a country experiences stability. A small principality that uses it will defend its territory, a great State that applies it will devour the empire. If the Tao has a beginning, it is nevertheless without end. The one who knows how to make use of it will achieve fullness; the one who does not know will hardly be able to make an impression. Whoever adheres to the Way will win fame; whoever follows it will endure throughout eternity. The ancient sages all put it into practice. The one who possesses it will understand the workings of Heaven and Earth, will penetrate the mysteries of demons and men. If he occupies a position in the army, the army will be [powerful]; if he is in charge of a country, the country will flourish. That is the reason why all sages in former times put this art into practice.

Rules of Conduct

Heaven has its unchanging branches, Earth its permanent laws. They act in concert with men, they form [one body] with the gods. Whoever is arrogant and expansive, whoever loves debate, plots harmful stratagems, and behaves like the rooster will be threatened with ruin. Whoever takes without giving will lose his country without delay. If he seizes what is near, seeks what is far, provokes hostile reactions, nurtures the seeds of sedition, he will only encounter pitfalls. Because Heaven does not like what is high, Earth what is vast, men what is rapacious. Whoever raises himself too high is reduced to dust by Heaven, whoever extends himself too far is broken by Earth, whoever demands too much is killed by men.

A man presents himself to me, I look him in the eye, his words correspond to his actions: I retain him and do not let him go; his words are flowery, his conduct pleasant: I keep him without giving him work. Words vouch for feelings, the facial expression is their flowering, the humors their back-wash. The one whose acts do not correspond to his discourse is a liar; conduct must follow through to the end what words set forth. Just as a straight tree is felled, a straight man is ready to die. Without form and without name, born before Heaven and Earth, he has not even begun to take form today.

The Way of Submission

The Yellow Emperor asked Power of the Pen:

"When Emperor Great Court* gained possession of the empire, the distinction between yin and yang was unknown, as were the movements of the sun and moon and the cycle of the season, yet Heaven dispensed its manna at the required time and Earth poured forth its riches. Why was that?"

---

*Mythic sovereign from earliest antiquity.

Power of the Pen:

"In his government, Great Court was calm and impassive. He took pains to maintain a gentle demeanor. Always respectful and shy, he remained withdrawn without ever putting himself forward. Benevolent, he was honest and inspired confidence; loving men, he proved affectionate and kind. Upright and valiant, he was careful of outranking others. Moderate in his appetites, he robbed no one and kept the One without demanding anything. He adopted the female stance in order to cultivate suppleness in himself. [. . .] the true virtue, because whoever loves virtue rejects strife. He confined himself to 'I do not dare,' and practiced 'I am unable.'* He wanted to reveal his hesitations and failings, and retaining the attitude of weakness, he strengthened himself. He watched for masculine behavior to be exhausted before subjecting his adversaries to his law.

"That is how his people worked without tiring, weathered shortages without ill effect, died without regrets in his armies. He did not exploit the masses, he was neither a warmonger, nor

---

*An idea found in section 67 of the *Lao Tzu*. A chapter in the cosmological encyclopedia *Lü-she ch'un-ch'iu*, compiled under the patronage of the prime minister of the king of Ch'in—the future Ch'in she-huang-ti—titled "Knowing the Standards," develops the related idea of "how to act?": "A monarch who knows the art of governing follows the course of things without ever acting, he observes without giving instructions. He banishes thoughts, forbids ideas. Calm, empty, he waits. He does not speak for his subjects; he does not take charge of their work. He observes the names, examines the facts, and the civil servants fulfill their duties by themselves. His principle is not knowing and his crown jewel 'how to act?' Yao said, 'How to act to extend the boundaries of your realm to the limits of the universe lit by the sun and moon?' Shun said, 'How to act to subdue the wild borders?' Yü the Great said, 'How to act to pacify the foreign countries where the Ching-pei, the Chiu-yang and the Ch'i-kung live?'"

a harbinger of unrest, nor a target for resentment; he did not plot dark schemes, he did not rashly decide dubious cases, he did not covet his neighbors' lands or houses. He watched over the masses, conforming to the rules of Heaven and Earth. He never took the initiative to act himself, but waited for adversaries to come to harm though the aberrations of their own behavior. When he noticed that Earth thwarted his efforts and that Heaven countered the seasons, he put things in order, so that he overcame through simplifying. Doing battle without exposing himself to vengeance, taking territories without provoking resistance, winning victories without even while enriching himself within, spreading his renown at hardly any cost: such are the results to expect from the way of submission."

> To possess the key to success and failure,
> examine forms and names.
> The forms establish themselves of their own accord,
> thus I am at rest.
> The tasks distribute themselves of their own accord,
> thus I have nothing to do.
> At rest and hidden,
> with nothing to move,
> the beings come forth of their own initiative
> and leave accordingly.

> Are you capable of concentration?
> Can you alone stop yourself?
> Do you know how to separate yourself from your ego
> and by yourself respect reason?

I am a bud, a hair,
I hardly exist:
things crowd toward me,
and I have an answer for everything.

I do not hold onto the old,
I do not cling to the past,
once gone, the new takes place.
As old and new do not mix,
I possess circular movement.

CANON III

APHORISMS

The Way consists of undertaking nothing but being content with responding. When an event has not yet taken place, it does not exist; once it has, conforming to it is enough. When a thing comes forth, it is manifested first by its form. One arranges for it according to this form and names it by its name. But how to name it?

When ministers repeatedly allow themselves one of these three offenses—undermining the sovereign's authority to promote their personal ambitions, flouting the law by giving free rein to their appetites, disturbing the smooth running of the government by preventing opinions from being expressed—it is not only himself that the prince will have trouble saving, but also his States.

Vice goes with vice and virtue with virtue; virtue and vice cannot live together.

The art of facing reversals in one's situation: diminish instead of growing, retreat rather than advancing. To arrive first is disastrous.

Whoever uses sights to aim will not commit errors; whoever uses a leveling rod to get his bearings will not go astray; whoever governs by applying the law will not experience troubles.

The sage does not take the initiative, he does not decide by himself, he does not hatch plans, he does not try to seize the advantage; he does not reject gifts from Heaven. He conforms to the order of things.

Whoever fails Heaven will perish, whoever deceives his master will suffer, whoever claims equal rank to his superior will kick himself.

Desires guide the will, the will guides our efforts. Thus, animals who live in nests worry about the wind, those who live in holes the rain; they worry about their survival. Whoever worries about his survival will enjoy security, whoever enjoys security will live a long time.

The emperor's ministers are called ministers, but they are really his masters; the king's ministers are called ministers, but they are really his friends; the hegemon's ministers are called ministers, but they are really his guests; the unstable ruler's ministers are called ministers, but they are really his servants;

the doomed sovereign's ministers are called ministers, but they are really his slaves.*

Whoever overextends himself will be dismembered. [. . .]; if he lives, his days will be threatened, if he dies, he will die in disgrace.

Respect the prohibitions when you take up your quarters, but do not choose propitious dates when you are cornered.†

A Son of Heaven does not have good ministers without hefty stipends, nor a general good soldiers without high pay, because men must believe that they are acting for themselves [and not that they are working for the interests of another.‡]

Do not renounce weapons; do not resort to them rashly. Under constraint, one can be obliged to make use of them.

Knowing what Heaven has in store and understanding the way Earth functions, the sage wholly embraces the laws of the universe; expansive is the vision of one who stands out in a crowd [. . .].

---

*A similar sequence appears in the first chapter of the *Ho Kuan Tzu*, "Wide Recruitment."

†This could also be understood as "Whoever takes shelter knows how to protect himself from danger, whoever is cornered does not know how to choose his moment."

‡A similar passage appears in the chapter "On Conformity" in the *Shan Tzu*, a work attributed to Shan Tao, statesman and political theoretician in the fourth century BCE. This passage is completed according to the parallel one.

The Son of Heaven's domain has an expanse of a thousand leagues on one side, that of a feudal prince only a hundred. That is what allows them to be interdependent. The feudal princes must not be equal to the Son of Heaven, the younger sons to the crown prince, the concubines to the chief wife. Confused, they try to harm each other, mixed up they collide.*

If the moment has come, respond immediately without another word; if the moment has not come, barricade your door without even sticking out your nose.

Heaven dispenses hot and cold, Earth governs high and low, man is free to take or give. Whoever gives and takes advisedly will be king, whoever gives and takes ill-advisedly will have to flee or be eliminated. Heaven reserves its punishment for him and he will draw misfortune down upon himself.

If, in a given epoch, ordinary methods prove ineffective, one can make use of his own insights rather than the Law; but he puts himself at risk and in peril as soon as he proves incapable of confronting the situation.

If a principality must endure, the empire cannot make it disappear. If it must disappear, the empire cannot preserve it.

As long as the opportunity has not presented itself, hide away

---

*There is a similar sequence in a chapter of the *Shan Tzu,* "On the Establishment."

and cultivate virtue; when you feel your time has come, make generous gifts and [do not spare] your efforts; once success is obtained, retrace your steps, so that no one will be able to take your place.

When the feudal princes do not suffer vengeance at each other's hands and do not avenge dishonors suffered, it is because there is [a sage].

The jealous, the envious, the deceitful: those are the kind of men that the prince must be careful to demote and to keep at distance, because if he does not keep them in subordinate positions and at a distance, they will soon see to inciting unrest.

One does not speak of public affairs with anyone incapable of controlling his women, nor of great subjects with anyone who neglects small things.

One must never hoard profits and collect bonuses: animals with horns do not have upper incisors.

One uses the pretext of a necessary restoration to punish a country, and once his goals are achieved, one ends the operation.

Nourishing grains have no flowers. Just words are not ornate, great joy does not bring laughter. Flowering plants necessarily bear fruit, all fruits contain pits; and in their pits there is a bitter-tasting kernel.

Here is the order commanded by the universe: I deploy my right and my left, I establish the masculine and the feminine; even though my actions are radiant, no one can follow the ins and outs of them; the wheels of my chariot are thunder and the team that draws it dragons; if advance is required, I move forward; if halting is required, I come to a halt. Earth is my base and men my guides. Whoever does not know how to conform to the terrain and to the human will accomplish nothing.*

The Emperor on High has an aversion to residences that exceed the standard. Also to the one for whom they are built who does not live in them, or only temporarily.

Limiting the luxuriousness of clothing and the comfort of bedding, reducing the thickness of the wood in caskets falls under the charge of prohibitions; in the case of an epidemic, authorization to drain ponds is stipulated by the prohibitions; in the case of mourning, authorization to cut trees in the mountains is stipulated by the prohibitions; collecting [. . .] leveling rises and filling depressions falls under the charge of the prohibitions; but they ought to be authorized in the case of flood.

Things must not come to be before their time; similarly plants must not flower before their season. Things realized too early soon come to ruin, flowers opening too early do not produce fruit.

---

*This description applies as much to the deployment of armies as to the cosmic movement. But in truth the two are consubstantial.

Sun marks day, moon night. One rises with the day and sleeps with the night. One must take care to respect Heaven's cycle and know to stop when it comes to its end.

The strong command, the weak obey; when there is equality, there is struggle, as if one applied the rope.

Even a father cannot demand that his sons show him love when his conduct inspires hate; a sovereign cannot require that his subjects show him respect when he deserves only contempt.

When a lineage is going to rise, it is as if one chops trees in [. . .]; when a lineage is going to fall, it is as if one chops trees on a mountain. When an honest and upright man comes to a premature end, he owes it to the unsettled misdeeds of his ancestors. If a raging madman achieves old age, it is because he benefits from the virtue of his ancestors.

What is low and straight will rise, what is high and bent will fall.

When a mountain bears trees, they are dense and luxuriant. However ferocious tigers are, they can be tamed. But it is difficult for brothers who share quarters to live on good terms. They cannot agree to live together but cannot bear to be apart, to the point that they undermine the spirits of their ancestors. [. . .] Why not try then to raise them in such a way as to instill gentleness? But can brotherly feelings be altered?

There are three certain causes of death in the world. The one who allows himself fits of passion without conserving his strength will perish, the one who gives free rein to his appetites will perish, the one with only weak forces at his disposal, who dares to confront those with large forces, will perish.

One does not lend weapons to a crook, one does not offer grain to his enemy. Because to lend weapons to a crook and to offer grain to an enemy is to reinforce the weak, to make the tiny grow, and in the end one prompts a role reversal that can be fatal.

Ordinarily, when the dissimilar becomes similar, it is the hand of man that has made it similar; when the similar becomes dissimilar, it is the hand of man that has made it dissimilar. But to obtain a spontaneous result with no intervention, one must know how to strive by following the course of things.

To show friendship when one feels hatred is called being all honey outside and all venom inside. A country where the nobles nurture such feelings will be threatened with enemies at the borders, if it does not experience internal unrest. Only when one shows friendship when he feels friendship and shows aversion when he feels aversion will a country be free from trouble within and threats from without.

Whoever finds something does not think he has been gratified; whoever loses something does not feel resentment [. . .].

The sun does not shine to lavish its light on men because it would be sorry to plunge them into darkness; thus, when men open their doors and their windows to take the light, the sun does not intervene at all. The Earth does not lavish its riches to protect men from destitution. Thus, when men cut trees and harvest grasses to procure what they need, the Earth does not intervene at all.*

When disturbances arise in a principality and when the one charged with intervening militarily to restore order adopts conduct counter to the law and moral code, it often happens that the country experiencing the trouble turns against him and makes him suffer the treatment that he inflicted on it. And if the circumstances make success impossible, there are sons and grandsons who will take responsibility for bringing this mission to a successful end. That is why it is said: "Whoever flouts celestial laws when charged with suppressing others will be suppressed by others."

The living have houses, the dead tombs. Because they must not attend to the same affairs.

Whoever, being lost, quickly retraces his steps, will not have too long a journey.

When two ministers have the same rank, the country is in peril; if, despite everything, the country is spared, that is due to the

---

*This sequence also appears in the "On Authority" chapter in the *Shan Tzu*.

sovereign's arbitration. But when the prince disappears and disorder threatens, if, despite the prince's disappearance, the realm remains intact, it is because the ministers still know how to respect rank. If two sons enjoy the same consideration within a family, it is in peril, unless the father intervenes to maintain its cohesion. But when the father is no longer there, its stability is threatened unless the other brothers observe precedence.*

The prince who neglects the assistance of his ministers and refuses to follow the advice of his wise councilors counts only on the strength of his walls and the bravery of his soldiers and exposes his person; a sovereign who exposes his person puts himself in danger. He can neither defend himself against solid resistance nor win a raging battle.

When two tigers fight, a mangy dog gets the better of the survivor.†

When one runs a State, the best is not having to apply punishments; next is [. . .]; after that is letting men settle their quarrels in brawls or lawsuits; the worst is forbidding brawls and lawsuits so that men can no longer settle their differences. The best consists of outdoing [. . .], then outdoing clear-sightedness, and finally mending one's ways.

---

*A similar text appears in the chapter "On the Establishment" in the *Shan Tzu.*

†There is a related proverbial expression, drawn from an anecdote in *Strategies of Royal Combatants:* "Watching tigers fight from the top of a mountain," in which it is a man who takes advantage of the fight between two wildcats.

Whoever acts as though it were summer in the middle of winter and in the middle of a heat wave acts as though it were winter puts his days in danger because he acts counter to the natural cycle.

Respect overcomes idleness, resolution doubt. The misfortune of a country doomed to ruin [. . .] does not believe in [. . .] nor in its impossibility, that is why it cannot be. And it does not believe in [. . .]. Thanks to examining past events one can understand the law of return. That is why [. . .] one considers the straight and the curved, and according to their qualifications, one evaluates and decides. Speculators are known to amass goods in order to profit from them, anticipating the opportune moment. Thus, to know how to govern, one examines whomever a sovereign employs, as one would look into amassed merchandise to anticipate the reversal of circumstances [. . .].

In any evaluation, one must have knowledge of the two great emblems that are yin and yang. Heaven is yang, Earth is yin; spring is yang, autumn yin; summer is yang, winter yin; day is yang, night yin; a great principality is yang, a small one yin; a powerful country is yang, a weak one yin; a busy man is yang, an idle one yin; what expands is yang, what retracts is yin; the sovereign is yang, the minister yin; the superior yang, the inferior yin; man yang, woman yin; father yang, son yin; the eldest son yang, the youngest son yin; the oldest yang, the youngest yin; the nobles yang, the commoners yin; success yang, misfortune yin; marriage and birth yang, mourning yin; to rule is yang, to be ruled is yin; the occupier is yang, the occupied yin;

the master is yang, the student is yin; speech is yang, silence is yin; to give is yang, to receive yin.

Everything that is yang has Heaven for a model, everything that is yin Earth. Heaven values rectitude, all that is distant from it is false [. . .] and arriving at its end is overturned. All that is yin is modeled on the Earth. The Earth's qualities are calmness, slowness, rectitude, rest; its attitude is flexibility and its essential concern stability. It gives without ever contesting. Such are the laws that govern Earth and such is female behavior.

CANON IV

THE ORIGINAL WAY

Within the immutable Origin governed a whirling entity, immense and void. This hollow immensity fused into a single body, one and the same. This single tumultuous body was closed, healed over itself, a humid, foggy dream—no light. Spiritual subtlety filled everything. In the quintessential calm, no light shone.

No action, no movement. The ten thousand things had not yet formed. The great whirlwind is ineffable.

Heaven did not cover. Earth did not bear. And nevertheless, it was already there: the primordial Tao, more subtle than the infinitely small, more vast than the infinitely large.

It extends between the four seas, it embraces the beyond. Humidity does not rot it, heat does not burn it because it is the source. Immutable cause of all the transformations, its breath inspires the flight of birds, the running of four-legged animals, the swimming of fish. All living beings exist in it and through it. It realizes all things.

All possess it, none know its name. There is no one who makes use of it, no one who knows its form. One is only a nickname, void only a container, non-action only a modality, harmony only a technique.

The supreme Tao is so high that no one can contemplate it, so deep that no one can sound it. The sunlight is only a weak expression of its brilliance, infinity does not capture its expanse. It is the One over which nothing has a hold.

Heaven and Earth, yin and yang, the four seasons, the sun and moon, the stars and planets, the clouds and wind, the insects that fly and that crawl, all that lives draws from its sap without diminishing it. All return to it without increasing it. It is hard without being brittle, it is tender and flexible and yet it does not bend. The atom is not smaller nor the universe more vast.

Only the sage can apprehend the formless, hear what has no sound, know the fullness of the void and make himself empty. He understands what is most secret in the universe; he forms one body with the first identity so closely that no crack divides them. He accumulates without ever increasing.

The one who submits to this discipline becomes eminently sharp. His intuition allows him to achieve the furthest limit of perception. He returns to the immeasurable, grasps the ungraspable.

If a sage king uses it, he will obtain the empire, he will profit from all, good and evil, without letting himself be abused. Empty and calm: men are peaceful. He establishes the correct principles: talent is recognized, the multitude without desires. He becomes the people's destiny, all believe him, no unrest troubles them.

The universe is in order, governed, perfect. Each is in its place, none compete, all have the necessary qualifications, the positions are well defined. Without orders, without exhortations, the people work themselves to death and die on the job. He does not seek to achieve great things: they come about of themselves. He does not need to lead inquiries: the most secret affairs spontaneously reach him.

Immobile, the sage holds the One. Knowing the Tao: extending little to embrace much, keeping to the straight way to rectify deviations, apprehending the future, the present, the past through the intuition of origins. Encompassing the One, establishing the Norm, he will unify the universe. Contemplating ancient times, he will grasp the historic necessity, and in what is still not yet the nothing, he will rediscover what already is.

INDEX